COLORFUL QUILTS

A JOURNEY THROUGH FABRIC

Cynthia LeBlanc Regone

Martingale®
& C O M P A N Y

Colorful Quilts: A Journey through Fabric
© 2007 by Cynthia LeBlanc Regone

That Patchwork Place® is an imprint of Martingale & Company®.

Martingale & Company
20205 144th Ave. NE
Woodinville, WA 98072-8478
www.martingale-pub.com

Printed in China
12 11 10 09 08 07   8 7 6 5 4 3 2 1

Library of Congress Cataloging-in-Publication Data
Library of Congress Control Number:
2006035740

ISBN: 978-1-56477-701-0

Credits

CEO: Tom Wierzbicki

Publisher: Jane Hamada

Editorial Director: Mary V. Green

Managing Editor: Tina Cook

Developmental Editor: Karen Costello Soltys

Technical Editor: Darra Williamson

Copy Editor: Melissa Bryan

Design Director: Stan Green

Illustrator: Laurel Strand

Cover and Text Designer: Shelly Garrison

Photographer: Brent Kane

Mission Statement

Dedicated to providing quality products
and service to inspire creativity.

Dedication

- To Carl, a great husband and father, who always finds the time to help and has given me 30 years of untold freedom to pursue my interests.

- To my children, John, Jennifer, and David, who have complete confidence in my ability to be a master at my craft.

- And to my mother, Joyce Margaret Gale LeBlanc, who started me on this journey when she came home with fabric remnants for me to make doll clothes, oh so long ago.

Acknowledgments

I would like to thank two shop owners who have been instrumental in advancing my career as a quiltmaker-teacher-lecturer: Nancy Mullman of The Cotton Patch in Tulsa, Oklahoma, and Terri Burton of Quilt 'N Sew in Katy, Texas.

Profound thanks to Betty Terrell, who taught me the fundamentals of quiltmaking.

Special thanks to Florence Brown, Elizabeth Nelson, and Gloria Greenlee for doing exchange blocks that were out of their "comfort zone." A special thank-you also to Gloria Greenlee for sharing the vintage Basket block pattern. She continues to be a generous and kind friend.

And to my quilting friends in Oklahoma, Texas, and beyond: thank you for 25 years of support and encouragement.

CONTENTS

A Quiltmaker's Journey

I have been sewing since I was a little girl. I sewed clothes for my Barbie doll, some of my school clothes, my prom dresses, and my wedding dress. I never dreamed that quilting, rather than dressmaking, would become such a major part of my life. My journey began in 1981 with my first quilting class. "The rest," as they say, "is history." I no longer sew clothes; in fact, I hate sewing on a button and I've been known to take my pants elsewhere to be hemmed. Everything changed for me when I made that first queen-size sampler quilt. Quilting became a passion.

Each quilt that I make takes me on a journey. Whether it's achieving accuracy in piecing, working with unusual fabric combinations, perfecting my appliqué stitches, or being open-minded about using a new computer program for quilters, it's all a journey worth taking over and over.

Traveling is also a great passion of mine . . . if only in my imagination. If each quilt I make represents a journey, then so is the process of creating it. Must I go to a particular place or region to know firsthand what it looks like? Absolutely not!! A quilt design can materialize from a photograph or with the discovery of the perfect fabric to duplicate my vision.

"A Walk in Provence" (page 30) is just that type of quilt. The border fabric spoke to me of beautiful flowering fields and crisp sunny days in the French countryside. "Bali High" (page 52) evokes visions of glorious sunsets and sparkling beaches in the tropics. "Birdhouses of Key West" (page 14) captures the South and the beautiful painted homes along the boule-vards. "Cherry-Picking Time" (page 44) can be enjoyed year-round without ever traveling to Washington State to pick a single cherry. What highway trip would be complete without stop-ping to pick a few wildflowers? "Black-Eyed Susans" (page 22) bloom effortlessly on this quilt and require little maintenance. Gather a group of friends to make two great exchange quilts, "Tropical Summer Baskets" (page 10) and "Razzle-Dazzle Cactus Baskets" (page 62). Do you have a collection of double-pink reproduction prints? "Double-Pink Blooms" (page 56) is a great scrap quilt for those fabrics that you have been saving.

Join me on this quilt journey as we travel the roads and byways for unusual fabric combi-nations, great patterns, better piecing skills, and colorful quilts.

The Right Fabric, the Perfect Quilt

The fabric makes the quilt. That's my story and I'm sticking with it.

When you look at a quilt, what catches your eye first? The fabric, right? After that initial glance, you might notice the blocks, the workmanship, and the quilting designs. But it's the fabric that stands out and makes you want to take a closer look. Choosing the right fabric for each quilt project is so important.

After 25 years of quilting, I still get excited over each project. My favorite part of quilting is collecting the fabrics to be used in the design. It may take me two years or more to accumulate just the right combination of fabrics, but the rewards are priceless. Here are a few tips on choosing the right fabrics to make the quilt projects in this book.

Selecting Key Fabrics

Often I am asked by my students, "Which comes first—the fabric or the design?" Making a quilt is like building a house: it starts with a sound foundation. Sometimes the design comes first, but that was not the case with "A Walk in Provence" (page 30). For this quilt, the colorful striped border fabric was the foundation that started my creative juices flowing. I carried a sample of the border print to as many quilt shops and shows as I could to collect fabrics for this quilt. Because the border print included so many colors, it was easy to pull fabrics together to make this project. When I had enough varieties of yellows, greens, blues, and reds, I was ready to start the quilt.

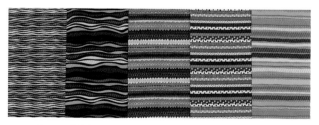

Striped fabrics make good foundation fabrics. Look for a stripe with three or more colors. This gives you multiple choices for coordinating fabrics.

Try experimenting with backgrounds. Gone are the days when cream, off-white, and white were our only choices. Spice up your quilts with color by choosing backgrounds that are tone-on-tone but not too busy. (I find lime green to be a great neutral. Don't you agree?) Study the examples below. Avoid using stripes, large checks, and other geometric designs as backgrounds for pieced blocks. These directional fabrics are just too distracting.

Good choices for backgrounds

Poor choices for backgrounds

High contrast is the key to making these quilts work. Don't be afraid to mix prints in the blocks and in the borders. You'll notice that I've mixed checks, stripes, dots, and florals in several of my quilts and borders, but the colors are all compatible with the foundation fabric. Keep scale in mind, particularly when picking fabrics to use in small pieced blocks. Larger-scale prints will be lost when the pieces are cut.

Don't be afraid to mix stripes, checks, florals, and other prints in your quilts.

The Power of Black and White

If you like working with bright colors, you'll love combining them with black-and-white prints. Black-and-white fabrics have become signature pieces in my designs. I buy them at almost every quilt shop I visit; they all go together. For example, "Razzle-Dazzle Cactus Baskets" (page 62) has more than 20 different white-with-black prints as backgrounds for the blocks. The key was to use prints with white backgrounds and small-scale black motifs so the fabrics read primarily as white rather than black. Most of the bright fabrics are small-scale prints, too.

Black-and-white prints are crisp and fresh in a quilt top. Consider them for an outer border or, as in the case of "Birdhouses of Key West" (page 14), as an inner border. This quilt top is very busy, so I used the black-and-white pieced border to "stop the motion" and give your eye a place to rest. Without that inner border, your eyes would never focus on the birdhouses or the appliquéd outer border. The quilt would be just a jumble of colors.

Scrap Quilts and More

I love scrap quilts! They are truly my favorite quilts to make. Almost all the quilts in this book are scrap quilts, and "Double-Pink Blooms" (page 56) is no exception. Granted, this is not a bright quilt, and it has absolutely no black-and-white fabrics in it, but it is a scrap quilt. Every once in a while I need to do something different, and I find working with reproduction prints to be soothing and restful. I have a large stash of these prints and usually use them in exchange projects with my friends, so putting together this quilt was not difficult. The pink stripe was my foundation fabric. "Oh," you might say, "there is only one color in the stripe." Yes, this is true, but I was able to capitalize on that color by adding soft greens, blues, reds, and more pinks because they all go together. It gave me an opportunity to use those double-pink reproduction prints that I had been saving for years. I added quite a few other reproduction fabrics and collected as many green prints for the Star block backgrounds as I could find. The double-pink half-square triangles needed those soothing greens to frame the appliquéd baskets.

To make scrap quilts, you need a stash. Not everyone has a built-in stash of black and white fabrics, brights, or reproduction prints. If you don't have a large stash of fabrics and want one in a hurry, buy bundles already packaged for you. These can be found at quilt shops and at the vendor's booths at quilt shows. Some fabric manufacturers create "towers" that feature a complete line of fabrics, and you can buy a variety of colors and prints in one package. This is a great way to start a stash or supplement your collection.

Collecting prepackaged bundles is a great way to build your fabric stash.

If scrap quilts are my favorite, you can imagine that two-color quilts are almost impossible for me to make. I also do not have a great love for batiks; they simply are not my favorite type of fabric to buy. In fact, I tell my friends that it puts me into a temporary coma when I buy batiks in earth tones. (Just kidding!!!) But in "Bali High" (page 52), I forced myself to work with batiks. (You might notice that I chose jewel tones rather than earth tones.) For this quilt I needed fabrics that read as solids as well as those with multiple colors to use as foundation fabrics. The solid or tone-on-tone prints coordinated with the multicolored batiks, giving me many color combinations to work with in the blocks. This quilt gave me an opportunity to buy lots of fat quarters and build up my stash. Aren't we always looking for an excuse to buy more fabrics?

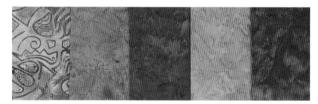

Batiks—both multicolored and those that read as solids—are the foundation for my quilt "Bali High."

That said, once in a while a design requires only a few fabrics for maximum impact, such as in "Black-Eyed Susans" (page 22) and "Cherry-Picking Time" (page 44). Keeping the fabric choices to a minimum gives these quilts a fresh, crisp look. Once again, a mixture of prints—checks, plaids, dots, and stars—was used to keep the quilts from being too predictable and boring.

Fabric Shopping Guidelines

As a teacher, lecturer, and designer, I am asked certain questions all the time.

- **How much fabric should I buy?** If you love a fabric and you think it would be great for a border, buy 3 yards. If you love the fabric but aren't sure what you are going to do with it, buy 2½ yards. If it would make a good background, buy at least 2 to 3 yards. If the fabric is on sale and would make a good backing, buy 6 yards. If it is a stripe (and you know how much I love stripes!), buy 2 to 3 yards. Buy fat quarters of blacks, whites, and brights . . . lots of fat quarters.

- **Should I wash my fabrics?** I know I am going to regret this one day, but my answer is usually no, although I do wash hand-dyed and red fabrics, especially if I am using the reds with white.

A Few Final Words

I would like to share a few final thoughts before you begin.

- Haste makes waste. I have learned this lesson over and over. I tell my students, "Making a quilt is not a race." Take a deep breath and enjoy the process.

- Measure, measure, measure, and then cut.

- Know how to read your rulers.

- Invest in a ¼" sewing foot.

- Take classes from as many different teachers as possible. Each can teach you the tricks that she or he has learned along the way.

- Try something different when choosing fabrics.

- Look for good foundation pieces. These fabrics can be stripes, florals, and prints. The fabrics should have many colors in the print.

- Most of all, enjoy the journey.

TROPICAL Summer Baskets

This cheerful quilt will brighten any room in your home. I exchanged the blocks with three friends who live many miles away. They had never used bright fabrics in their quilt blocks before and found the exchange a challenge and a joy.

Materials

Yardage is based on 42"-wide fabric unless otherwise noted.

2⅛ yards of yellow tone-on-tone print for block backgrounds, alternate blocks, and setting triangles

2⅛ yards of black print for outer border and binding

½ yard of multicolored stripe for middle border

⅜ yard of blue check for inner border

7" x 7" square *each* of 35 assorted bright tone-on-tone prints for basket points and bases

3" x 3" square *each* of 35 assorted bright prints for baskets

3 yards of fabric for backing

56" x 70" piece of batting

Cutting

Measurements include ¼" seam allowances. Cut all strips on the crosswise grain (selvage to selvage) unless otherwise noted.

From the yellow tone-on-tone print, cut:

2 strips, 3¾" x 42"; crosscut into 18 squares, 3¾" x 3¾". Cut each square twice diagonally to yield 72 quarter-square triangles. You will have 2 triangles left over.

8 strips, 1¾" x 42"; crosscut into:
35 squares, 1¾" x 1¾"
70 rectangles, 1¾" x 3"

2 strips, 3⅜" x 42"; crosscut into 18 squares, 3⅜" x 3⅜". Cut each square once diagonally to yield 36 half-square triangles. You will have 1 triangle left over.

4 strips, 5½" x 42"; crosscut into 24 squares, 5½" x 5½"

2 squares, 4½" x 4½"; cut each square once diagonally to yield 4 half-square triangles

2 strips, 8⅜" x 42"; crosscut into 5 squares, 8⅜" x 8⅜". Cut each square twice diagonally to yield 20 quarter-square triangles.

From *each* 7" x 7" bright tone-on-tone square, cut:

3 squares, 2⅛" x 2⅛"; cut each square once diagonally to yield 6 half-square triangles (210 total)

From the blue check, cut:
8 strips, 1¼" x 42"

From the multicolored stripe, cut:
7 strips, 2" x 42"

From the *lengthwise grain* of the black print, cut:
2 strips, 4½" x 54"
2 strips, 4½" x 68"
4 strips, 2½" x 72"

Finished quilt size: 48⅝" x 62⅞"   Finished block size: 5" x 5"

Making the Blocks

1. Sew a matching bright half-square triangle to each short edge of a small yellow quarter-square triangle; press. Make 70 in matching pairs.

Make 70
in matching pairs.

2. Sew a 1¾" yellow square to a unit from step 1 as shown; press. Sew the matching unit from step 1 to a 3" bright print square; press. Sew the units together; press. Make 35.

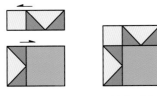

Make 35.

3. Sew a remaining bright half-square triangle to a 1¾" x 3" yellow rectangle as shown; press. Make 35 of each in matching pairs.

Make 35 each
in matching pairs.

4. Sew matching units from step 3 to the matching unit from step 2 as shown; press. Make 35.

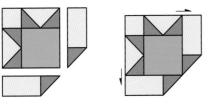

Make 35.

5. Finger-press the center of each small yellow half-square triangle. Match the center of a creased triangle with the bottom center of

each basket unit; pin. Sew and press. Square up the block to 5½" x 5½". Make 35 blocks.

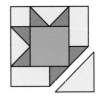

Make 35.

Don't Second Guess!

Never guess at the center of a triangle; you might be wrong. Instead, take the time to fold the triangle and finger-press the center. You'll always know exactly where the center is.

Assembling the Quilt

1. Arrange the Basket blocks, the 5½" yellow squares, and the large yellow side (quarter-square) and corner (half-square) setting triangles in diagonal rows as shown in the assembly diagram. Sew the blocks, squares, and triangles together into rows; press.

2. Pin and sew the rows together, carefully matching the seams; press.

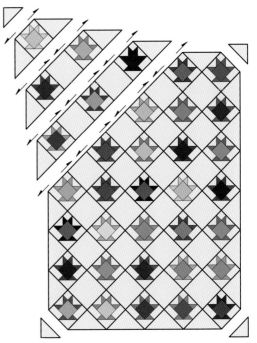

Assembly diagram

Adding the Borders

1. Sew the 1¼"-wide checked strips together end to end to make one long strip. Press the seams open. From this strip, cut two strips that measure 1¼" x 54" and two strips that measure 1¼" x 68". Repeat with the 2"-wide striped strips.

2. Sew a 1¼" x 54" checked strip, a 2" x 54" striped strip, and a 4½" x 54" black strip together along their long edges to make a border unit as shown; press. Make two. Repeat using the 68"-long checked, striped, and black strips.

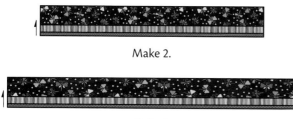

Make 2.

Make 2.

3. Referring to "Borders with Mitered Corners" on page 74, sew the 54"-long border units to the top and bottom of the quilt and the 68"-long border units to the sides; press. Miter the corners.

Quilt plan

Finishing the Quilt

Refer to "Finishing" on page 75 as needed to complete the quilt.

1. Piece the backing as needed. Layer the quilt top with batting and backing; baste.

2. Machine or hand quilt as desired.

3. Square up the quilt "sandwich." Use the 2½"-wide black strips to bind the quilt edges. Finish by adding a label to the back of the quilt.

Guidelines for a Successful Block Exchange

Here are a few simple steps to follow if you are planning to make and exchange blocks with a group of quilting friends.

- Select a leader from the participants committed to the group project.
- Choose a block suitable for the skill level of your group.
- Determine a reasonable time schedule for the exchange. Anticipate that some blocks may be tardy, and plan to be flexible.
- Determine the total number of blocks each participant will make.
- Decide whether blocks should be signed or not.
- If incorporating appliqué into your block, choose a form of appliqué that will suit everyone in the exchange.
- Pick a common fabric to be used within the block or as the background.
- Try something new when choosing fabrics for the blocks.
- Always use good-quality, 100%-cotton fabric.
- Do your best work. Measure and trim your blocks before you submit them.

Remember: you want to remain friends during and after the block exchange!

BIRDHOUSES of Key West

Throw care to the wind when choosing fabrics for this breezy wall hanging. Mix bright pink with orange, purple with red, or use any combination involving high contrast to create one-of-a-kind birdhouses. What bird wouldn't love to build its nest in such a colorful home?

Materials

Yardage is based on 42"-wide fabric unless otherwise noted. Fat quarters measure 18" x 22"; fat eighths measure 9" x 22".

Fat eighth *each* of 9 assorted bright small-scale background prints for blocks*

Large scrap *each* of 36 assorted bright small- to medium-scale prints for birdhouses

¾ yard of blue-and-green stripe for binding

½ yard of blue-and-green floral print for outer border

½ yard of large-scale tropical floral print for border appliqués

⅜ yard of green print for middle border

¼ yard of black solid for inner border and birdhouse hole appliqués

¼ yard of white solid for inner border

Scraps of blue, yellow, pink, and green solids and 2 circular prints for snail appliqués

1⅝ yards of fabric for backing

38" x 56" piece of batting

Freezer paper

1 yard of lightweight fusible web

1 yard of tear-away stabilizer

Black, blue, yellow, pink, and green thread or embroidery floss

Approximately 200 small-diameter gold beads (optional)

Avoid bold stripes.

Cutting

Measurements include ¼" seam allowances. Cut all strips on the crosswise grain (selvage to selvage) unless otherwise noted.

From *each* assorted fat eighth of bright small-scale background print, cut:
1 strip, 4½" x 22"; crosscut into 2 strips, 4½" x 7" (18 total; pieces 6 and 8)

1 strip, 2½" x 22"; crosscut into:
  1 strip, 2½" x 9" (9 total; piece 2)
  1 strip, 2½" x 8" (9 total; piece 3)

From the assorted scraps of bright small- and medium-scale prints, cut a *total* of:
9 rectangles, 5" x 9" (piece 1)
9 squares, 3" x 3" (piece 4)
18 strips, 2" x 10" (pieces 5 and 7)

From the black solid, cut:
2 strips, 2½" x 42"

From the white solid, cut:
2 strips, 2½" x 42"

Finished quilt size: 30½" x 48½" • Finished block size: 6" x 12"

From the green print, cut:
4 strips, 2½" x 42"; crosscut into:
   2 strips, 2½" x 38½"
   2 strips, 2½" x 24½"

From the blue-and-green floral print, cut:
4 strips, 3½" x 42"

From the blue-and-green stripe, cut:
2½"-wide bias strips to total approximately 170"*

Refer to "Cutting and Making Bias Strips," step 1, on page 72.

Foundation Piecing 101

Here are a few tips to make foundation piecing effortless.

- Keep the following tools beside your sewing machine: a small rotary cutter, cutting mat, and pressing surface; a wooden ruler or small crafter's iron for pressing; and a small ¼" and/or ⅛" ruler for trimming seams.

- Before making multiple copies of the pattern, make one photocopy and place it over the original to test for accuracy. If there are any distortions, trace the pattern on lightweight paper instead.

- Make extra copies of foundation patterns. Mistakes do happen and it's nice to have extras on hand.

- When in doubt, cut the fabric *at least* 1" larger than the pattern piece.

- Use a larger-than-normal needle—9/14, for example—in your machine.

- Sew with a neutral-colored thread.

- Set your machine for smaller stitches than usual—for example, 15 to 18 stitches per inch. This will make it so much easier to remove the foundation paper later.

- Use a dry iron. Do not press directly on the paper; the ink may come off on your iron and ironing surface.

- Remove the foundation paper as directed one section at a time. If you have difficulty removing the paper, fold the perforated edge back and forth a few times. That should sufficiently weaken the paper to facilitate removal.

Making the Blocks

Make each block using a single background fabric for pieces 2, 3, 6, and 8 and four different bright small- and medium-scale prints for pieces 1, 4, 5, and 7.

1. Make nine photocopies of the birdhouse pattern on page 20. Trim each pattern on the outer dotted line.

2. Place fabric piece 1 right side up over section 1 on the unprinted side of the foundation pattern; pin. Turn the pattern over and hold it up to a light source to make sure at least ¼" of the fabric piece extends beyond all sides of section 1. Adjust if necessary.

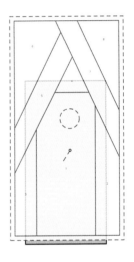

3. Place fabric piece 2 right sides together with fabric piece 1; pin. Fold fabric piece 2 open to make sure it will completely cover section 2, including a ¼" seam allowance, when sewn. Adjust if necessary.

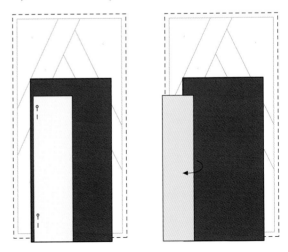

4. Turn the pattern over and stitch on the line between sections 1 and 2, starting and ending ¼" beyond the line. Fold fabric 2 open and finger-press.

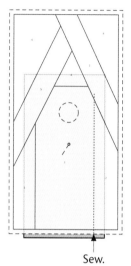

Sew.

5. Refold fabric 2 and fold the paper foundation back to expose the seam allowance. Place your ruler along the edge of the foundation and trim the seam allowance to ¼".

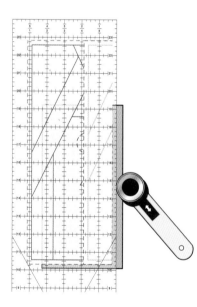

6. Continue in the same manner to add the remaining fabric pieces in numerical order. Finger-press and trim after each addition. Trim the finished block on the dotted pattern line to measure 6½" x 12½". You can remove the paper now or after you have pieced the quilt top.

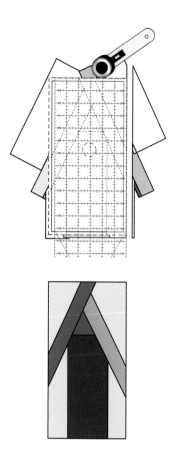

7. Repeat steps 2–6 to make a total of nine Birdhouse blocks.

8. Use the pattern on page 20 to make a template for the birdhouse hole. Referring to "Freezer-Paper Hand Appliqué" on page 70, use the black fabric and freezer paper to prepare nine birdhouse hole appliqués for hand appliqué. Use matching thread and an invisible stitch to appliqué a birdhouse hole to each birdhouse.

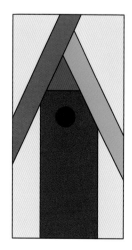

Assembling the Quilt

1. Arrange the Birdhouse blocks in three horizontal rows of three blocks each as shown in the assembly diagram. Pay close attention to color placement for a pleasing, color-balanced layout. Sew the blocks together into rows; press.

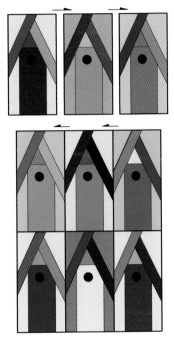

Assembly diagram

2. Pin and sew the rows together, carefully matching the seams. If you haven't removed the foundation papers, do so now; press. The quilt top should measure 18½" x 36½".

Adding the Borders

1. Sew a 2½" x 42" black strip and a 2½" x 42" white strip together to make a strip set as shown; press. Make two. Cut the strip sets into 28 segments, 1½" wide.

1½"

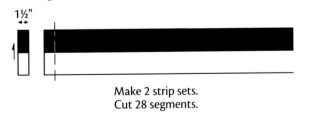

Make 2 strip sets.
Cut 28 segments.

2. Sew nine segments from step 1 together; press. Make two units for the side inner borders.

Side border.
Make 2.

3. Sew five segments from step 1 together; press. Make two units for the top and bottom inner borders.

Top/bottom border.
Make 2.

4. Referring to the quilt plan below, sew the border units from step 2 to the sides of the quilt. Press the seams away from the border units. Sew the border units from step 3 to the top and bottom; press.

5. Sew the 2½" x 38½" green strips to the sides of the quilt. Press the seams toward the newly added border. Sew the 2½" x 24½" strips to the top and bottom; press.

6. Sew the 3½"-wide blue-and-green floral strips together end to end to make one long strip. From this strip, cut two strips that measure 3½" x 42½" and two strips that measure 3½" x 30½".

7. Sew the 3½" x 42½" floral strips to the sides of the quilt. Press the seams toward the newly added border. Sew the 3½" x 30½" strips to the top and bottom; press.

Quilt plan

Additional Appliqués and Embellishments

1. Use the patterns on page 21 to make templates for the snail (body, accent, and shell). Referring to "Fusible Appliqué" on page 71, use the blue, yellow, pink, green, and circular print scraps to prepare two sets (one regular and one reverse) of snail appliqués for fusing. Refer to the manufacturer's instructions and the photo on page 15 to fuse the prepared appliqués to the quilt top. Finish the appliqué edges with matching thread and a hand or machine buttonhole stitch. Refer to "Basic Embroidery Stitches" on page 75 as needed.

Experiment with Appliqués

If you prefer, substitute birds, bugs, or butterflies for the snail appliqués.

2. Select a few large flowers and leaves from the large-scale tropical floral print and use the fusible web to prepare them for fusing. Refer to the manufacturer's instructions and the photo to fuse the prepared appliqués to the quilt top. Pin a single layer of tear-away stabilizer to the wrong side of the border fabric, beneath the appliqués. Finish the appliqué edges with matching thread and a narrow machine satin stitch. Remove the stabilizer and press the borders.

"Free" the Flowers

Don't limit yourself to staying within the borders when grouping the flowers. Spilling them into the quilt top adds interest to your design.

3. For extra sparkle, stitch small gold beads to the center of the appliquéd flowers. After each bead is added, make a small knot on the wrong side of the fabric behind the bead so that the beads are securely anchored.

Finishing the Quilt

Refer to "Finishing" on page 75 as needed to complete the quilt.

1. Piece the backing as needed. Layer the quilt top with batting and backing; baste.

2. Machine or hand quilt as desired.

3. Square up the quilt "sandwich." Use the 2½"-wide blue-and-green striped strips to bind the quilt edges. Finish by adding a label to the back of the quilt.

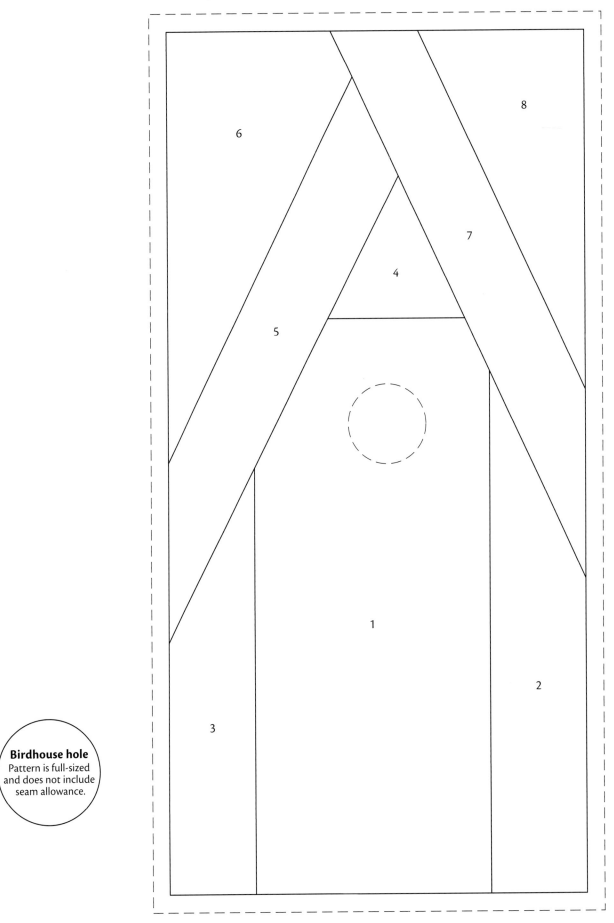

6

8

7

4

5

1

2

3

Birdhouse hole
Pattern is full-sized
and does not include
seam allowance.

BIRDHOUSES OF KEY WEST

Birdhouse foundation pattern
Enlarge 133%.

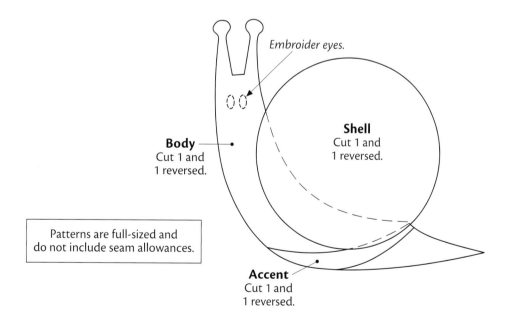

Embroider eyes.

Shell
Cut 1 and
1 reversed.

Body
Cut 1 and
1 reversed.

Patterns are full-sized and
do not include seam allowances.

Accent
Cut 1 and
1 reversed.

Black-Eyed SUSANS

What could be more enjoyable to piece than a fabric garden of bright yellow starflowers? Add a few appliquéd hearts and you have a delightful quilt to brighten any room.

Materials

Yardage is based on 42"-wide fabric.

2¼ yards of black-with-white dotted print for outer border, sashing of Heart blocks, Flower blocks, and background of border Star blocks

1½ yards of black-and-white check for background of Heart blocks and sashing of Flower blocks

1⅛ yards of green solid for heart and leaf appliqués, flower stems, and inner border

⅞ yard of red solid for heart appliqués and middle border

⅞ yard of red-with-black dotted print for Flower blocks

⅝ yard of yellow solid for Flower blocks and border Star blocks

⅝ yard of black-and-white stripe for binding

3¼ yards of fabric for backing (horizontal seam)

64" x 79" piece of batting

2 yards of lightweight fusible web

Freezer paper

2 yards of tear-away stabilizer

¼"-wide bias pressing bar

Red and green embroidery floss or thread

5½ yards of jumbo yellow rickrack

Fabric sizing

Cutting

Measurements include ¼" seam allowances. Cut all strips on the crosswise grain (selvage to selvage).

From the black-and-white check, cut:
3 strips, 10" x 42"; crosscut into 13 rectangles, 7" x 10"

12 strips, 1½" x 42"; crosscut into:
    24 strips, 1½" x 9½"
    24 strips, 1½" x 8½"

From the green solid, cut:
3 strips, 1¼" x 42"; crosscut into 12 strips, 1¼" x 7"

6 strips, 1½" x 42"

From the black-with-white dotted print, cut:
26 strips, 1½" x 42"; crosscut into:
    26 rectangles, 1½" x 9½"
    26 rectangles, 1½" x 8½"
    48 rectangles, 1½" x 2½"
    48 squares, 1½" x 1½"
    24 rectangles, 1½" x 4½"
    24 rectangles, 1½" x 6½"

5 strips, 6½" x 42"

From the red-with-black dotted print, cut:
11 strips, 1½" x 42"; crosscut into:
    48 rectangles, 1½" x 2½"
    48 squares, 1½" x 1½"
    24 rectangles, 1½" x 9½"

2 strips, 4½" x 42"; crosscut into 12 rectangles, 4½" x 5½"

Quilted by Sharon Dixon
Finished quilt size: 56½" x 71½" • Finished block size: 8" x 11"

From the yellow solid, cut:

8 strips, 1½" x 42"; crosscut into 192 squares, 1½" x 1½"

2 strips, 2½" x 42"; crosscut into 24 squares, 2½" x 2½"

From the red solid, cut:

6 strips, 1½" x 42"

From the black-and-white stripe, cut:

7 strips, 2½" x 42"

Making the Heart Blocks

The background blocks have been cut ½" larger than necessary and will be trimmed to size when the appliqué is complete.

1. Fold each 7" x 10" check rectangle in half vertically and horizontally to find the center of the block; finger-press.

2. Use the patterns on page 29 to make templates for the large and small hearts. Referring to "Fusible Appliqué" on page 71, use the green solid to prepare 13 small heart appliqués and the red solid to prepare 13 large heart appliqués for fusing.

3. Position a red heart in the center of a creased rectangle from step 1. Center a green heart in the red heart. Refer to the manufacturer's instructions to fuse the prepared appliqués to the block. Make 13.

4. Pin a single layer of tear-away stabilizer to the wrong side of each block. Make sure the stabilizer covers the entire area of the appliqué design. Finish the appliqué edges with matching thread and a machine buttonhole stitch. Remove the stabilizer, press, and trim each block to 6½" x 9½". If you prefer to use

a hand buttonhole stitch, omit the stabilizer and refer to "Basic Embroidery Stitches" on page 75 as needed.

5. Sew an appliquéd block between two 1½" x 9½" black dotted rectangles; press. Sew a 1½" x 8½" black dotted rectangle to the top and bottom; press. Trim the block to 8½" x 11½". Make 13 blocks.

Make 13.

Making the Flower Blocks

1. Draw a diagonal line on the wrong side of 96 of the 1½" yellow squares. With right sides together, align a marked yellow square with one end of a 1½" x 2½" red dotted rectangle. Stitch directly on the diagonal line. Trim ¼" beyond the sewn line; press. Repeat to add another marked square to the opposite end of the rectangle as shown. Make 36. Set the remaining marked squares aside for now.

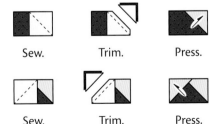

Sew. Trim. Press.

Sew. Trim. Press.
Make 36.

2. With wrong sides together, fold a 1¼" x 7" green strip in half lengthwise. Sew a ⅜" seam allowance from the raw edge of the folded strip. Trim, leaving a ⅛" seam allowance. Make 12.

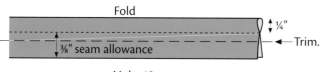

Fold

¼"

⅜" seam allowance ←— Trim.

Make 12.

3. Insert the ¼"-wide bias pressing bar into the tube, centering the seam on the back. Press the strip with fabric sizing to stabilize it, and remove the bar. Repeat with all 12 strips.

←— ¼" bias bar

Make 12.

4. Position a strip from step 3 in the center of a remaining 1½" x 2½" red dotted rectangle as shown; pin in place. Repeat step 1 using the remaining marked 1½" yellow squares to make a flying-geese unit as shown. *Do not* trim the green strip. Make 12.

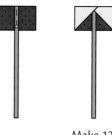

Make 12.

5. Sew a unit from step 1 between two 1½" red dotted squares as shown; press. Repeat, substituting a unit from step 4 for the unit from step 1; press. Make 12 of each.

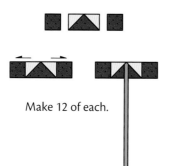

Make 12 of each.

6. Sew a 2½" yellow square between two remaining units from step 1; press. Make 12.

Make 12.

7. Sew a unit from step 6 between one of each unit from step 5 as shown; press. Make 12.

Make 12.

8. Fold up the stem of a unit from step 7, right sides together. Sew a 4½" x 5½" red dotted rectangle to the bottom of the unit; press. Make 12.

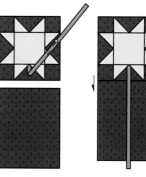

Pin stem out of the way.   Make 12.

9. Sew each unit from step 8 between two 1½" x 9½" red dotted strips; press. Make 12.

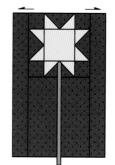

Make 12.

10. Use the patterns on page 29 to make templates for the leaf and the flower center. Referring to "Freezer-Paper Hand Appliqué" on page 70, use the green fabric and freezer paper to prepare 24 leaf appliqués (12 regular and 12 reversed) and the black dotted fabric and freezer paper to prepare 12 flower centers for hand appliqué. Use matching thread and an invisible stitch to appliqué the stem and one flower center to each block as shown. Trim the end of the stem even with the raw edge of the unit. Make 12.

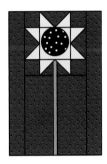

Make 12.

11. Sew a unit from step 10 between two 1½" x 9½" checked rectangles; press. Sew a 1½" x 8½" checked rectangle to the top and bottom; press. Use matching thread and an invisible stitch to appliqué one of each leaf from step 10 to the block. Make 12 blocks.

Make 12.

Assembling the Quilt

1. Arrange the Heart and Flower blocks in five horizontal rows of five blocks each, alternating the blocks as shown in the assembly diagram. Sew the blocks together into rows; press.

2. Pin and sew the rows together, carefully matching the seams; press. The quilt top should measure 40½" x 55½".

Assembly diagram

3. Cut two 40½"-long strips and two 55½"-long strips of yellow rickrack. Align a 40½"-long strip of rickrack with the top raw edge of the quilt. Use matching thread to topstitch the rickrack in place as shown. Repeat to add the remaining 40½" piece of rickrack to the bottom, and the 55½"-long pieces to the sides. Press the quilt top.

Adding the Borders

1. Sew the 1½"-wide green border strips together end to end to make one long strip; press. From this strip, cut two strips that measure 1½" x 40½" and two strips that measure 1½" x 57½".

2. Sew the 1½" x 40½" strips to the top and bottom of the quilt. Press the seams toward the borders. Sew the 1½" x 57½" strips to the sides; press.

3. Sew the 1½"-wide red solid border strips together end to end to make one long strip; press. From this strip, cut two strips that measure 1½" x 42½" and two strips that measure 1½" x 59½".

4. Sew the 1½" x 42½" strips to the top and bottom of the quilt. Press the seams toward the newly added border. Sew the 1½" x 59½" strips to the sides; press.

Making and Adding the Star Border

1. Referring to step 1 of "Making the Flower Blocks" on page 24, use the remaining 1½" yellow squares and the 1½" x 2½" black dotted rectangles to make 48 flying-geese units. Sew a flying-geese unit between two 1½" black dotted squares; press. Make 24.

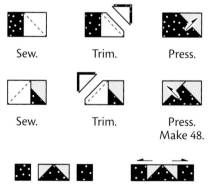

Sew.   Trim.   Press.

Sew.   Trim.   Press.
Make 48.

Make 24.

2. Sew a 2½" yellow square between two remaining flying-geese units; press. Make 12.

Make 12.

3. Sew each unit from step 2 between two units from step 1 as shown; press. Make 12 star units.

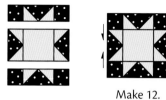

Make 12.

4. Sew a unit from step 3 between two 1½" x 4½" black dotted rectangles; press. Sew a 1½" x 6½" black dotted rectangle to the top and bottom; press. The block should measure 6½" x 6½". Make 12 border Star blocks.

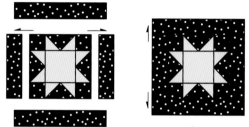

Make 12.

5. Sew the 6½"-wide black dotted border strips together end to end to make one long strip; press. From this strip, cut two strips that measure 6½" x 47½" and two strips that measure 6½" x 32½".

6. Sew a Star block from step 4 to each end of a 6½" x 47½" black dotted strip from step 5 as shown. Press the seams toward the strip. Make two. Referring to the quilt plan on page 28, sew a border unit to the left and right edges of the quilt. Press the seams toward the newly added border.

Side border.
Make 2.

7. Sew two Star blocks from step 4 to each end of a 6½" x 32½" black dotted strip from step 5; press. Make two and sew them to the top and bottom of the quilt; press.

Top/bottom border.
Make 2.

Finishing the Quilt

Refer to "Finishing" on page 75 as needed to complete the quilt.

1. Piece the backing as needed. Layer the quilt top with batting and backing; baste.

2. Machine or hand quilt as desired.

3. Square up the quilt "sandwich." Use the 2½"-wide black-and-white striped strips to bind the quilt edges. Finish by adding a label to the back of the quilt.

Quilt plan

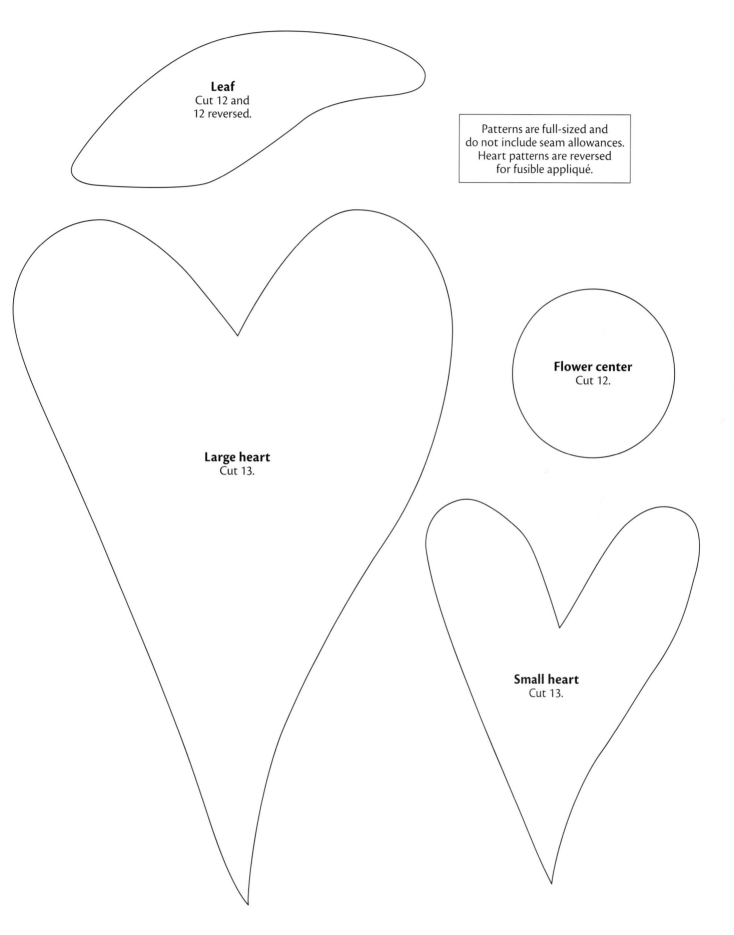

Leaf
Cut 12 and
12 reversed.

Patterns are full-sized and
do not include seam allowances.
Heart patterns are reversed
for fusible appliqué.

Flower center
Cut 12.

Large heart
Cut 13.

Small heart
Cut 13.

A Walk in PROVENCE

Take a trip to the lush countryside of southern France without leaving home. Start your journey with a collection of royal blue, mustard yellow, and deep red fabrics and combine them to make this stunning row quilt.

Materials

Yardage is based on 42"-wide fabric unless otherwise noted. Fat quarters measure 18" x 22"; fat eighths measure 9" x 22".

2 yards of striped border print for outer border

⅜ yard of red check for row 3

⅜ yard of blue plaid for row 7

Fat quarter *each* of 7 assorted mustard yellow prints for rows 1, 2, 3, 5, 8, and 10; beehives; and flowers

Fat quarter *each* of 6 assorted royal blue prints for rows 3, 5, 6, 8, and 10 and flower centers

Fat quarter *each* of 6 assorted green prints for rows 3, 4, 5, 8 and 10; cherry leaves; and flower leaves

Fat quarter *each* of 6 assorted red prints for rows 2, 3, 5, 6, 8, 9, and 10; cherries; flowers; and hearts

Fat quarter of green solid, or ¼"-wide green Quick Bias Tape, for flower stems

Fat eighth *each* of 3 assorted brown prints for row 3, cherry vine, and beehive door

Fat eighth of black solid for birdhouse holes and bee bodies

3" x 10" square of white solid for bee wings

1" x 5" scrap of yellow solid for bee bodies

½ yard of dark blue print for binding

3⅛ yards of fabric for backing (horizontal seam)

56" x 65" piece of batting

Black and brown embroidery floss

6" x 6" square of lightweight fusible web

6" x 6" square of tear-away stabilizer (optional)

¼"-wide bias pressing bar

Silver or chalk pencil

Cutting

Measurements include ¼" seam allowances. Cut all strips on the crosswise grain (selvage to selvage) unless otherwise noted.

ROW 1: CHERRY-VINE APPLIQUÉ

From *each* assorted mustard yellow print, cut:
1 rectangle, 4½" x 6" (7 total)

From assorted brown print 1, cut:
1¼"-wide bias strips to total 30"*

Finished quilt size: 48½" x 57½" • Finished row length: 36"

ROW 2: CHECKERBOARD

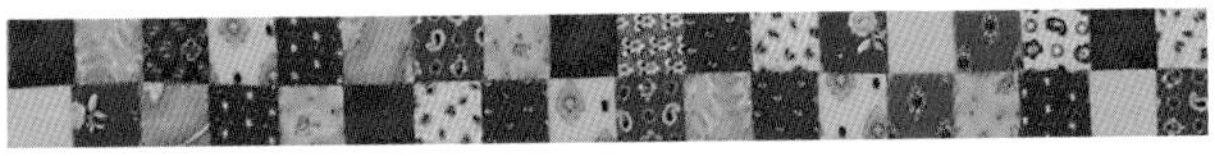

From *each* assorted red print, cut:
6 squares, 1½" x 1½" (36 total)

From *each* of 6 assorted mustard yellow prints, cut:
6 squares, 1½" x 1½" (36 total)

ROW 3: BIRDHOUSES

From the red check, cut:
6 squares, 3⅞" x 3⅞"; cut each square once diagonally to yield 12 half-square triangles

12 pieces, 2¼" x 2½"

12 strips, 1½" x 6½"

From *each* assorted royal blue print, cut:
1 square, 3⅞" x 3⅞"; cut once diagonally to yield 2 half-square triangles (12 total)

From assorted brown print 2, cut:
6 strips, 1" x 2½"

From the assorted green prints, cut a *total* of:
2 squares, 4½" x 4½"

From the assorted mustard yellow prints, cut a *total* of:
2 squares, 4½" x 4½"

From the assorted red prints, cut a *total* of:
2 squares, 4½" x 4½"

ROW 4: HALF-SQUARE TRIANGLES

From *each* assorted green print, cut:
3 squares, 2⅞" x 2⅞"; cut once diagonally to yield 6 half-square triangles (36 total)

ROW 5: BASKETS

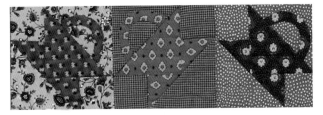

From *each* of 2 assorted mustard yellow prints, cut:
1 square, 4⅞" x 4⅞"; cut once diagonally to yield 2 half-square triangles (4 total) for background

2 squares, 2½" x 2½" (4 total), for background

From 1 assorted royal blue print, cut:
1 square, 4⅞" x 4⅞"; cut once diagonally to yield 2 half-square triangles for background

2 squares, 2½" x 2½", for background

From *each* of 2 assorted green prints, cut:
1 square, 4⅞" x 4⅞"; cut once diagonally to yield 2 half-square triangles (4 total) for background

2 squares, 2½" x 2½" (4 total), for background

From 1 assorted red print, cut:
1 square, 4⅞" x 4⅞"; cut once diagonally to yield 2 half-square triangles for background

2 squares, 2½" x 2½", for background

From *each* of 2 assorted royal blue, green, and red prints, cut:
1 square, 4⅞" x 4⅞"; cut once diagonally to yield 2 half-square triangles (12 total) for baskets. You will have 1 triangle left over in each print.

1 square, 2⅞" x 2⅞"; cut once diagonally to yield 2 half-square triangles (12 total) for baskets

ROW 6: FLYING GEESE

From 1 assorted royal blue print, cut:
72 squares, 1½" x 1½"

From 1 assorted red print, cut:
36 rectangles, 1½" x 2½"

ROW 7: BEEHIVE APPLIQUÉ

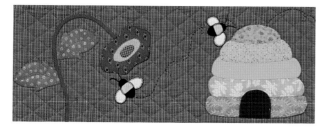

From the blue plaid, cut:
1 strip, 9½" x 37½"

From the green solid, cut:
2 bias strips, 1¼" x 15" (or 2 strips, 15" long, of
¼"-wide green Quick Bias Tape)*

From the black solid, cut:
2 strips, 1" x 5"

ROW 8: HEART BLOCKS

From *each* of 3 assorted red prints, cut:
4 squares, 2½" x 2½" (12 total)

**From the assorted mustard yellow prints, cut a
total of:**
5 squares, 4½" x 4½"
4 matching squares, 2½" x 2½"

From *each* of 2 assorted royal blue prints, cut:
1 square, 4½" x 4½" (2 total)
4 matching squares, 2½" x 2½" (8 total)

From the assorted green prints, cut a *total* of:
2 squares, 4½" x 4½"
12 squares, 2½" x 2½", in matching sets of 4

ROW 9: RED PRINT CHECKERBOARD

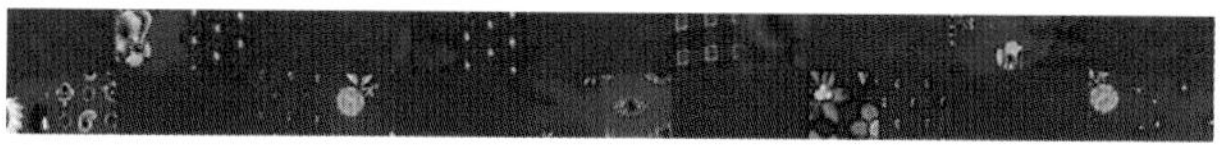

From 5 of the assorted red prints, cut a *total* of:
36 squares, 1½" x 1½"

From the remaining assorted red print, cut:
18 rectangles, 1½" x 2½"

ROW 10: STARFLOWER BLOCKS

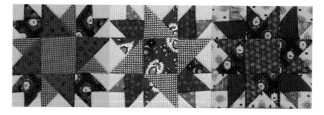

Each Starflower block uses a different mustard
yellow print and green print for the background
and half-square "leaf" triangles. The starflower
in each block is made from a different combination of three royal blue and/or red print fabrics in
a contrasting value. Before cutting, study the quilt
photo on page 31 and plan the combination for
each of the blocks.

From *each* of 6 assorted mustard yellow prints, cut:
8 squares, 1½" x 1½" (48 total)
2 squares, 1⅞" x 1⅞"; cut each square once diago-
    nally to yield 4 half-square triangles (24 total)
1 square, 3¼" x 3¼"; cut twice diagonally to yield 4
    quarter-square triangles (24 total)

From *each* assorted green print, cut:
2 squares, 1⅞" x 1⅞"; cut each square once diago-
    nally to yield 4 half-square triangles (24 total)

From the assorted red prints, cut a *total* of:
12 rectangles, 1½" x 2½", in matching sets of 4
3 squares, 3¼" x 3¼"; cut each square twice diago-
    nally to yield 12 quarter-square triangles**
6 squares, 2⅞" x 2⅞", in matching pairs; cut each
    square once diagonally to yield 12 half-square
    triangles in matching sets of 4
3 squares, 2½" x 2½"**

From the assorted royal blue prints, cut a *total* of:
12 rectangles, 1½" x 2½", in matching sets of 4
3 squares, 3¼" x 3¼"; cut each square twice diago-
    nally to yield 12 quarter-square triangles**
6 squares, 2⅞" x 2⅞", in matching pairs; cut each
    square once diagonally to yield 12 half-square
    triangles in matching sets of 4
3 squares, 2½" x 2½"**

*Refer to "Cutting and Making Bias Strips," step 1, on
    page 72.*

**Cut these in matching sets of one 2½" square and four
    quarter-square triangles.*

BORDERS AND BINDING

From the *lengthwise grain* of the border stripe, cut:

2 strips, 6½" x 54"

2 strips, 6½" x 64"

From the dark blue print, cut:

5 strips, 2½" x 42"

Making Row 1: Cherry-Vine Appliqué

1. Sew the seven 4½" x 6" yellow print rectangles together along the short edges as shown; press.

2. Referring to "Cutting and Making Bias Strips" on page 72, use the 1¼"-wide brown print 1 bias strips to make a 30"-long bias vine, piecing if necessary. Sew ⅜" from the raw edge of the folded strip. Trim, leaving a ⅛" seam allowance.

3. Fold the vine in half crosswise and finger-press to mark the center. Repeat using the background unit from step 1. Pin the vine to the background unit in a gentle curve, placing the vine at least 1" from the top edge and matching the centers. Turn under each end of the vine approximately ¼" and appliqué the vine to the background using matching thread and an invisible stitch.

4. Use the patterns on page 42 to make templates for the cherry leaf and cherries. Referring to "Freezer-Paper Hand Appliqué" on page 70, use the assorted green prints and freezer paper to prepare 10 leaf appliqués (5 regular and 5 reversed) and the assorted red

prints and freezer paper to prepare 5 large cherries and 10 small cherries for hand appliqué. Referring to the photo on page 31, use matching thread and an invisible stitch to hand appliqué 5 leaf-and-cherry clusters (1 of each leaf, 1 large cherry, and 2 small cherries) along the vine.

Perfect Circles, Every Time

To make tracing circles easier, use a circle template found at any office supply shop. Your circles will be perfectly round and the same size each time you trace them.

5. Use a silver or chalk pencil to draw cherry stems for each leaf-and-cherry cluster on the background as shown on the pattern. Use two strands of brown embroidery floss and a stem stitch to embroider the stems. Refer to "Basic Embroidery Stitches" on page 75 as needed. Press and trim the row to 4½" x 36½".

Making Row 2: Checkerboard

Sew 18 of the 1½" assorted red print squares and 18 of the 1½" assorted yellow print squares together, alternating them as shown to make a row; press. Make two. Sew the rows together, orienting them as shown; press. The row should measure 2½" x 36½".

Make 2.

Making Row 3: Birdhouses

1. Sew a 3⅞" red checked half-square triangle and a 3⅞" assorted blue print half-square triangle together to make a half-square-triangle unit as shown; press. Make two matching units. Sew the units together as shown; press.

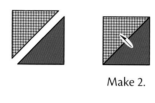

Make 2.

2. Sew a 1" x 2½" brown print 2 strip between two 2¼" x 2½" red checked pieces; press.

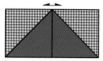

3. Sew a 4½" assorted green, yellow, or red print square to a long edge of the unit from step 2; press. Sew the unit between two 1½" x 6½" red checked strips; press.

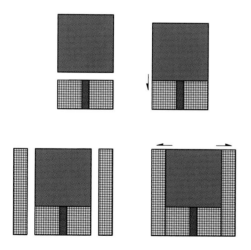

4. Sew the unit from step 1 to the top of the unit from step 3; press.

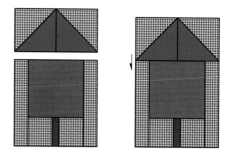

5. Repeat steps 1–4 to make a total of six blocks. The blocks should measure 6½" x 9½".

6. Use the pattern on page 42 to make a template for the birdhouse hole. Referring to "Fusible Appliqué" on page 71, use the black solid to prepare six birdhouse hole appliqués for fusing. Refer to the manufacturer's instructions to fuse a prepared appliqué to each birdhouse as shown. Finish the edges with decorative stitching.

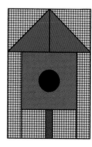

7. Trim 1½" or less from the bottom of one block from step 6. Cut a strip the same measurement *plus* ½" wide x 6½" long from the remaining red check. Sew the strip to the top of the block; press. The block should measure

6½" x 9½". Make four, using the blocks from step 6 and varying the width of the cut slightly from block to block.

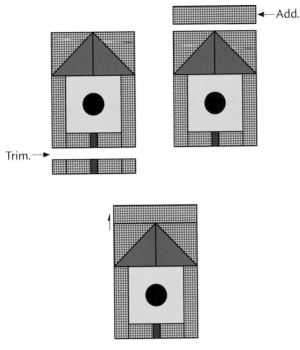

Make 4.

8. Arrange the Birdhouse blocks from steps 6 and 7 in a pleasing manner and sew them together to make a row as shown; press. The row should measure 9½" x 36½".

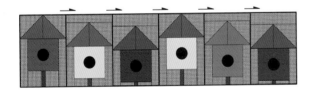

Making Row 4: Half-Square Triangles

1. Sew the 2⅞" assorted green print half-square triangles together in pairs to make half-square-triangle units as shown; press. Make 18.

Make 18.

2. Sew the units from step 1 together to make a row as shown; press. The row should measure 2½" x 36½".

Making Row 5: Baskets

1. Use the pattern on page 42 to make a template for the basket handle. Referring to "Freezer-Paper Hand Appliqué" on page 70, use an assorted red, royal blue, or green print that matches each basket and freezer paper to prepare six handles for hand appliqué.

2. Fold each handle in half and finger-press to mark the center. Mark the centers of the four 4⅞" yellow half-square background triangles, two 4⅞" royal blue half-square background triangles, four 4⅞" green half-square background triangles, and two 4⅞" red half-square background triangles. Referring to the photo on page 31 for color guidance, match the center of a creased background triangle with the center of each handle, aligning the bottom edges as shown; pin. Use matching thread and an invisible stitch to hand appliqué the handle to the triangle. Remove the freezer paper; press. Make six. Set the remaining creased triangles aside for now.

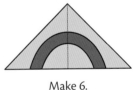

Make 6.

3. Sew each unit from step 2 to a 4⅞" *uncreased* red, royal blue, or green half-square basket triangle as shown; press. Square up each unit to 4½" x 4½". Make six.

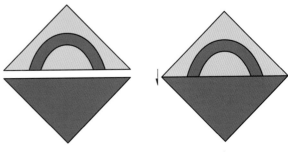

Make 6.

4. Sew a 2⅞" half-square triangle that matches the basket to a 2½" square that matches the background as shown; press. Make six of each in matching pairs.

Make 6 of each.

5. Sew each matching pair from step 4 to the matching unit from step 3 as shown; press. Match the center of a remaining, matching-colored, creased background triangle with the bottom center of the matching basket unit; pin. Sew and press. Square up the block to 6½" x 6½". Make six blocks.

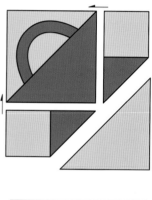

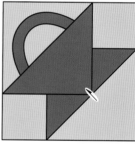

Make 6.

6. Sew the six Basket blocks together, turning them as shown to make a row; press. The row should measure 6½" x 36½".

Making Row 6: Flying Geese

1. Draw a diagonal line on the wrong side of each 1½" royal blue print square. With right sides together, align a marked blue square with one end of a 1½" x 2½" red print rectangle as shown. Stitch directly on the diagonal line. Trim ¼" beyond the sewn line; press. Repeat to add another marked square to the opposite end of the rectangle. Make 36.

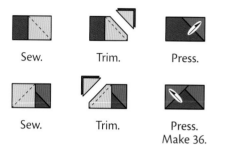

Sew.   Trim.   Press.

Sew.   Trim.   Press.
                  Make 36.

2. Sew 18 units from step 1 together along their long edges as shown; press. Make two.

Make 2.

3. Sew the rows from step 2 together, rotating one row as shown; press. The row should measure 2½" x 36½".

Making Row 7: Beehive Appliqué

The background strip has been cut 1" larger than necessary and will be trimmed to size when the appliqué is complete. Keep this in mind as you place the appliqués so that you do not overlap the seam allowances.

1. Use the patterns on pages 42 and 43 to make templates for the beehive (six pieces), flower (three pieces), and flower leaf. Referring to "Freezer-Paper Hand Appliqué" on page 70, use the assorted yellow prints to prepare the five beehive sections; brown print 3 to prepare the beehive door; one royal blue,

one yellow, and one red print to prepare two of each flower piece; and one green print to prepare four leaves (two regular and two reversed) for hand appliqué.

2. Fold the 9½" x 37½" blue plaid strip in half crosswise and finger-press to mark the center. Referring to the photo on page 31, layer and pin the beehive in the center of the strip. Use matching thread and an invisible stitch to appliqué the beehive sections and the beehive door in place. Remove the freezer paper as you go.

3. Referring to "Cutting and Making Bias Strips," on page 72, use the 1¼"-wide green bias strips to make two 15"-long bias stems. Sew ⅜" from the raw edge of the folded strips. Trim, leaving a ⅛" seam allowance. Using the photo as a guide, position and pin the stems in place, and use matching thread to hand appliqué them to the background.

4. Refer to the photo to layer and pin one of each flower piece and two leaves (one regular and one reversed) to each stem on the background strip. Use matching thread and an invisible stitch to appliqué the flowers and leaves in place. Remove the freezer paper as you go.

5. Sew the 1" x 5" scrap of yellow solid between the two 1" x 5" black solid strips to make a strip set as shown. Trim the seam allowances to ⅛"; press.

6. Use the patterns on page 42 to make templates for the bee body (one piece) and bee wings (two pieces). Referring to "Fusible Appliqué" on page 71, use the strip set from

step 5 to prepare three bee bodies and the square of white solid to prepare three sets of bee wings for fusing.

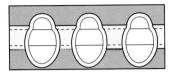

Refer to the manufacturer's instructions and the photo to fuse the prepared appliqués to the background strip as shown, making sure that the bodies overlap the wings by at least ⅛".

7. Pin a single layer of tear-away stabilizer to the wrong side of the background strip behind each bee. Make sure the stabilizer covers the entire area of the appliqué design. Finish the appliqué edges with black thread and a machine buttonhole stitch. Remove the stabilizer and press. If you prefer to use a hand buttonhole stitch, omit the stabilizer and refer to "Basic Embroidery Stitches" on page 75 as needed.

8. Referring to "Basic Embroidery Stitches" and the pattern, use two strands of black embroidery floss and a stem stitch to embroider antennae for each bee. Use a running stitch to show the bees' flight path around the flowers and beehive.

9. Press and trim the row to 8½" x 36½".

Making Row 8: Heart Blocks

1. Draw a diagonal line on the wrong side of each 2½" square of assorted red, yellow, blue, and green print. With right sides together and referring to the photo on page 31 for color guidance, align matching marked squares on opposite corners of a 4½" square of a contrasting yellow, blue, or green print. Stitch directly on the diagonal lines. Trim ¼" beyond the sewn lines; press. Repeat to add matching marked squares to the remaining corners. Square up the unit to 4½" x 4½". Make nine.

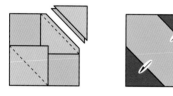

Make 9.

2. Use the pattern on page 42 to make a template for the heart. Referring to "Freezer-Paper Hand Appliqué" on page 70, use assorted red prints and freezer paper to prepare five hearts for hand appliqué. Referring to the photo, use matching thread and an invisible stitch to hand appliqué a heart to the center of five units from step 1.

3. Sew the units from steps 1 and 2 together to make a row, alternating them as shown; press. The row should measure 4½" x 36½".

Making Row 9: Red Print Checkerboard

1. Sew the 1½" assorted red print squares together in random pairs. Press the seam allowances toward the darker squares. Make 18.

Make 18.

2. Sew a 1½" x 2½" red print rectangle to each unit from step 1; press. Make 18.

Make 18.

3. Sew the units from step 2 together in pairs, taking care to orient the units as shown; press. The unit should measure 2½" x 4½". Make nine.

Make 9.

4. Sew the units from step 3 together as shown; press. The row should measure 2½" x 36½".

MAKING ROW 10: STARFLOWER BLOCKS

1. Sew a 1⅞" yellow print half-square triangle and a 1⅞" green print half-square triangle together to make a half-square-triangle unit as shown; press. Make four matching units.

Make 4.

2. Sew a half-square-triangle unit from step 1 to a matching 1½" yellow print square; press. Make four units.

Make 4.

3. Draw a diagonal line on the wrong side of the four remaining 1½" squares of the matching yellow print. Referring to the photo on page 31 for color guidance and with right sides together, align a marked yellow square with one end of a 1½" x 2½" red or blue print rectangle. Stitch directly on the diagonal line. Trim ¼" beyond the sewn line; press. Make four matching units.

Make 4.

4. Sew a unit from step 2 to a unit from step 3; press. Make four.

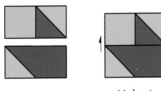

Make 4.

5. Referring to the photo, sew a matching 3¼" yellow quarter-square triangle to a short side of a 3¼" quarter-square triangle in a red or blue print that differs from the rectangle in the unit from step 3; press. Make four matching units.

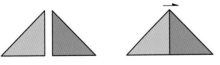

Make 4.

6. Referring to the photo, sew each unit from step 5 to a 2⅞" half-square triangle in a third different red or blue print; press. The unit should measure 2½" by 2½". Make four matching units.

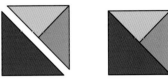

Make 4.

7. Arrange the units from steps 4 and 6 and a 2½" square that matches the quarter-square triangle in step 5 in three rows as shown. Sew the units and squares together into rows; press. Sew the rows together; press. Square up the block to 6½" x 6½".

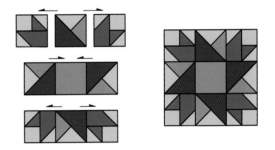

8. Repeat steps 1–7 to make a total of six blocks.

9. Sew the blocks together to make a row as shown; press. The row should measure 6½" x 36½".

Assembling the Quilt

1. Arrange rows 1–10 as shown in the quilt plan on page 41 or as desired. Sew the rows together; press. The quilt should measure 36½" x 45½".

2. Referring to "Borders with Mitered Corners" on page 74, sew the 6½" x 54" striped border strips to the top and bottom of the quilt and the 6½" x 64" striped border strips to the sides; press. Miter the corners.

Create a Border Stripe

I was very fortunate to find just the perfect striped fabric for the border of this quilt. If you cannot find a striped border to coordinate with the colors in your quilt, make your own fabric. Combine strips in varying widths from three different fabrics and piece them together. You now have a custom border that is perfect for your quilt top.

Finishing the Quilt

Refer to "Finishing" on page 75 as needed to complete the quilt.

1. Piece the backing as needed. Layer the quilt top with batting and backing; baste.

2. Machine or hand quilt as desired.

3. Square up the quilt "sandwich." Use the 2½"-wide dark blue strips to bind the quilt edges. Finish by adding a label to the back of the quilt.

Quilt plan

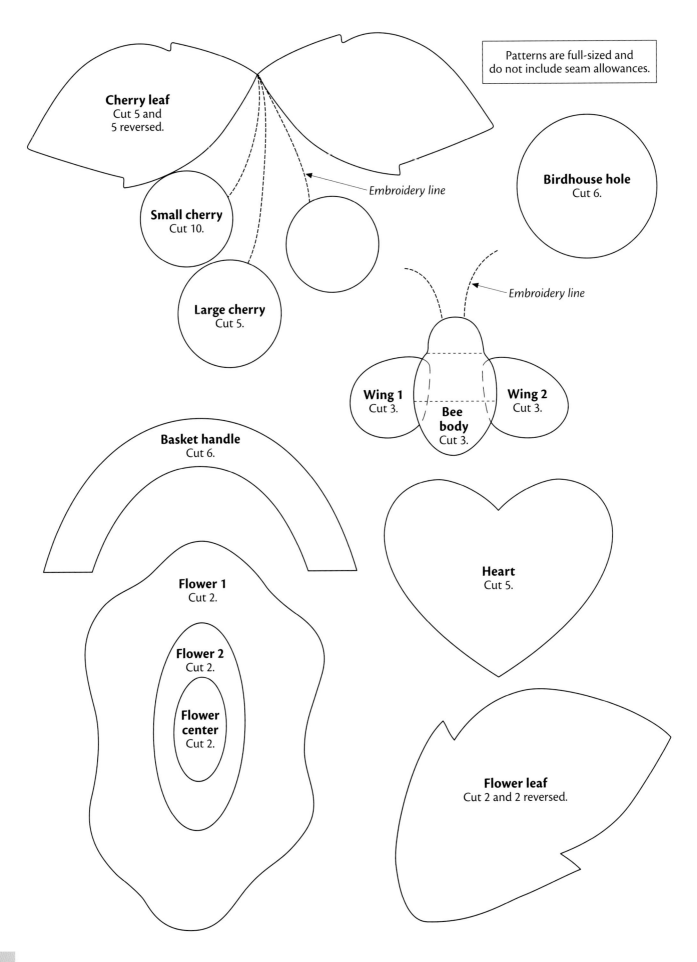

Patterns are full-sized and
do not include seam allowances.

Cherry leaf
Cut 5 and
5 reversed.

Embroidery line

Small cherry
Cut 10.

Large cherry
Cut 5.

Birdhouse hole
Cut 6.

Embroidery line

Wing 1
Cut 3.

Wing 2
Cut 3.

**Bee
body**
Cut 3.

Basket handle
Cut 6.

Heart
Cut 5.

Flower 1
Cut 2.

Flower 2
Cut 2.

**Flower
center**
Cut 2.

Flower leaf
Cut 2 and 2 reversed.

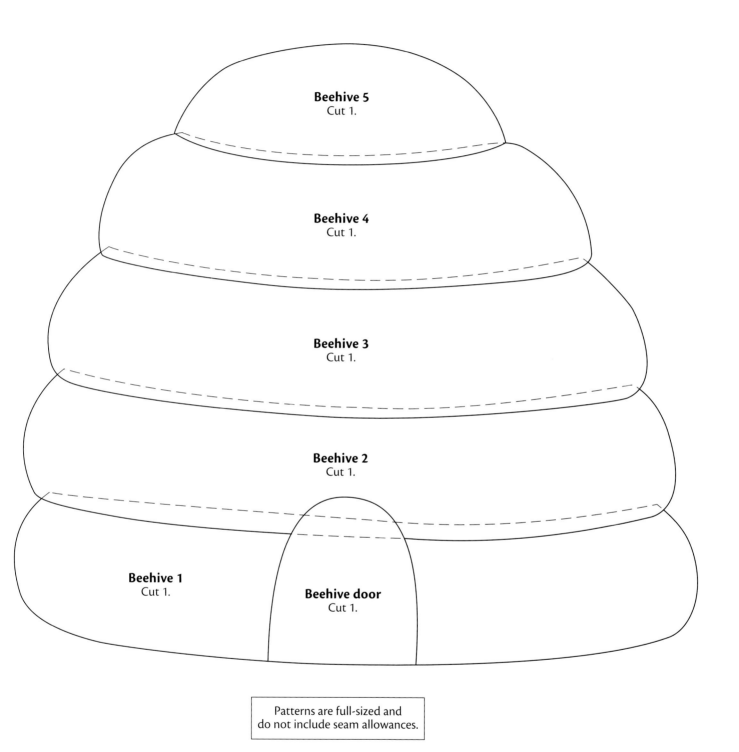

Beehive 5
Cut 1.

Beehive 4
Cut 1.

Beehive 3
Cut 1.

Beehive 2
Cut 1.

Beehive 1
Cut 1.

Beehive door
Cut 1.

Patterns are full-sized and
do not include seam allowances.

CHERRY-PICKING Time

What could be more reminiscent of summer than cherries ripe off the vine and baskets ready to collect them? Black, white, and red fabrics give this quilt—inspired by a vintage quilt block from the 1800s—a fresh, updated look. Cherry appliqués in the alternate blocks complete the cheerful design.

Materials

Yardage is based on 42"-wide fabric unless otherwise noted. Fat quarters measure 18" x 22"; fat eighths measure 9" x 22".

1⅞ yards of black cherry print for baskets, Cherry block cornerstones, setting triangles, borders, and binding

⅝ yard of white-with-red print for Basket and Cherry block backgrounds

½ yard of red check for baskets, Cherry blocks, and border triangles

¼ yard of red solid for flat piping accent

Fat eighth of brown solid, or ¼"-wide brown Quick Bias Tape, for bias stems

Fat eighth of green solid for leaves

8" x 8" square of red print for cherries

2⅓ yards of fabric for backing*

42" x 42" piece of batting

Green embroidery floss

¼"-wide bias pressing bar

*If your fabric measures a full 42" wide after the selvages are removed, you can reduce this to 1⅙ yards.

Cutting

Measurements include ¼" seam allowances. Cut all strips on the crosswise grain (selvage to selvage) unless otherwise noted.

From the black cherry print, cut:

3 strips, 2⅛" x 42"; crosscut into 41 squares, 2⅛" x 2⅛". Cut each square once diagonally to yield 82 half-square triangles. You will have 1 triangle left over.

1 strip, ⅞" x 42"; crosscut into 9 strips, ⅞" x 3½"

1 strip, 1½" x 42"; crosscut into 16 squares, 1½" x 1½"

2 squares, 9¾" x 9¾"; cut each square twice diagonally to yield 8 quarter-square triangles

2 squares, 5⅛" x 5⅛"; cut each square once diagonally to yield 4 half-square triangles

2 strips, 1¼" x 26"

2 strips, 1¼" x 27½"

3 strips, 2⅜" x 42"; crosscut into 38 squares, 2⅜" x 2⅜". Cut each square once diagonally to yield 76 half-square triangles

2 strips, 2" x 30½"

2 strips, 2" x 33½"

4 strips, 2½" x 42"

Finished quilt size: 34" x 34" • Finished block size: 6" x 6"

From the red check, cut:

2 strips, 2⅛" x 42"; crosscut into 27 squares, 2⅛" x 2⅛". Cut each square once diagonally to yield 54 half-square triangles.

2 strips, 1½" x 42"; crosscut into 16 strips, 1½" x 4½"

3 strips, 2⅜" x 42"; crosscut into 38 squares, 2⅜" x 2⅜". Cut each square once diagonally to yield 76 half-square triangles.

From the white-with-red print, cut:

3 strips, 1" x 42"; crosscut into 18 strips, 1" x 6"

1 strip, 2⅝" x 42"; crosscut into 5 squares, 2⅝" x 2⅝". Cut each square once diagonally to yield 10 half-square triangles. You will have 1 triangle left over.

1 strip, 6⅞" x 42"; crosscut into 5 squares, 6⅞" x 6⅞". Cut each square once diagonally to yield 10 half-square triangles. You will have 1 triangle left over.

1 strip, 4½" x 42"; crosscut into 4 squares, 4½" x 4½"

From the red solid, cut:

4 strips, 1" x 26"

From the brown solid, cut:

4 bias strips, 1¼" x 3½"*

4 bias strips, 1¼" x 3"*

Refer to "Cutting and Making Bias Strips," step 1, on page 72.

Making the Basket Blocks

1. Sew a 2⅛" black print half-square triangle and a 2⅛" checked half-square triangle together to make a half-square-triangle unit as shown; press. Make 45.

Make 45.

2. Arrange and sew three units from step 1 and three 2⅛" black print half-square triangles in diagonal rows as shown; press. Sew the rows together; press. Make nine.

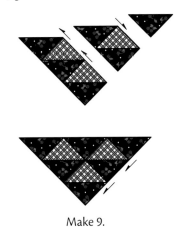

Make 9.

3. Align the lower-right corner of a 1" x 6" white print strip to the left edge of each unit from step 2 as shown. The strip will extend beyond the top edge of the unit. Sew the strip to the unit; press. Use a ruler and rotary cutter to trim the excess fabric; press. Make nine.

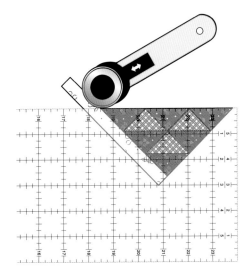

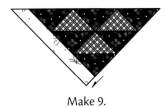

Make 9.

4. Arrange and sew together two remaining units from step 1 and one remaining 2⅛" black print half-square triangle; press. Make nine. Repeat step 3 to sew a 1" x 6" white print strip to the right edge of each unit. Press and trim.

Make 9.

5. Finger-press the center of a 2⅝" white print half-square triangle and a ⅞" x 3½" black print strip. Match the center of the creased triangle with the center of the strip; pin. Sew and press. Finger-press the center of a remaining 2⅛" checked half-square triangle. Match the center of the creased triangle to the previously sewn unit; pin, sew, and press. Square up the unit to 2¼" x 2¼". Make nine.

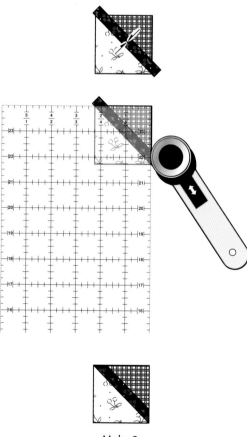

Make 9.

6. Sew a unit from step 5 to each unit from step 4 as shown; press. Make nine.

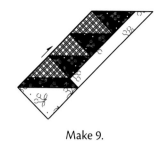

Make 9.

7. Sew each unit from step 6 to a unit from step 3 as shown; press. Make nine.

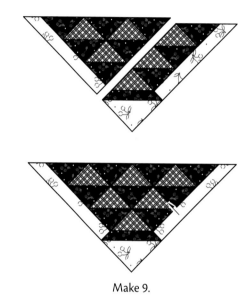

Make 9.

8. Use the pattern on page 51 to make a template for the basket handle. Referring to "Freezer-Paper Hand Appliqué" on page 70, use the black print and freezer paper to prepare nine handles for hand appliqué.

9. Fold each handle in half and finger-press to mark the center. Repeat with the 6⅞" white print half-square triangles. Match the center of a creased triangle with the center of each handle, aligning the bottom edges as shown on page 48; pin. Use matching thread and an

47

invisible stitch to hand appliqué the handle to the triangle. Remove the freezer paper; press. Make nine.

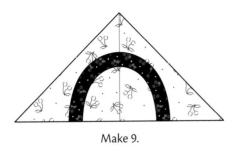

Make 9.

10. Sew a unit from step 9 to each unit from step 7 as shown; press. Square up the block to 6½" x 6½". Make nine blocks.

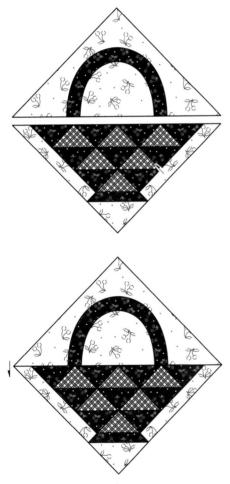

Make 9.

Making the Cherry Blocks

1. Sew a 4½" white print square between two 1½" x 4½" checked strips as shown; press. Make four.

Make 4.

2. Sew a 1½" black print square to each end of a remaining 1½" x 4½" checked strip; press. Make eight. Sew a unit to the top and bottom of each unit from step 1; press. Make four.

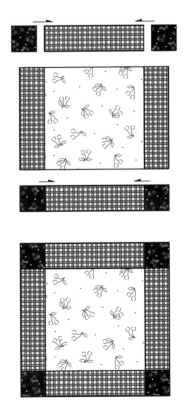

Make 4.

3. Refer to "Cutting and Making Bias Strips" on page 72 and use the 1¼"-wide brown strips to make bias stems. Sew ⅜" from the raw edge of the folded strip. Trim, leaving a ⅛" seam allowance. Make four of each.

4. Use the patterns on page 51 to make templates for the leaf and the large and small cherries. Referring to "Freezer-Paper Hand Appliqué," use the green fabric to prepare eight leaf appliqués (four regular and four reversed) and the red print square to prepare four large cherries and four small cherries for hand appliqué.

5. Referring to the diagram below, use matching thread and an invisible stitch to hand appliqué one of each stem from step 3, one of each leaf, and one large and one small cherry to each unit from step 2.

6. Use two strands of green embroidery floss and a stem stitch to embroider veins in the leaves as shown. Refer to "Basic Embroidery Stitches" on page 75 as needed.

Assembling the Quilt

1. Arrange the Basket blocks, the Cherry blocks, and the large black print side (quarter-square) and corner (half-square) setting triangles in diagonal rows as shown in the assembly diagram at top right. Sew the blocks and triangles together into rows; press.

2. Pin and sew the rows together, carefully matching the seams; press.

Assembly diagram

Adding the Borders

1. Fold one 1" x 26" red solid strip in half lengthwise, wrong sides together; press. Align the raw edges of the pressed strip with the raw edges of one side of the quilt top. Machine baste the piping in place, using a scant ¼" seam allowance and matching thread. Repeat for the remaining three sides of the quilt top.

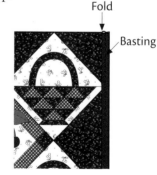

Fold

Basting

2. Sew the 1¼" x 26" black print border strips to the top and bottom of the quilt. Press the seams toward the borders, making sure the folded edge of the piping remains turned toward the quilt center. Sew the 1¼" x 27½" black print border strips to the sides; press.

3. Sew together a 2⅜" black print half-square triangle and a 2⅜" checked triangle as shown; press. Make 76.

Make 76.

4. Sew the units from step 3 together in pairs as shown; press. Make 36.

Make 36.

5. Sew eight units from step 4 and two remaining units from step 3 together to make a row as shown; press. Make two. Referring to the quilt plan below, sew one row to the top and one row to the bottom of the quilt. Press the seams toward the quilt center.

Top/bottom border.
Make 2.

6. Sew ten units from step 4 together to make a row as shown; press. Make two and sew them to the sides of the quilt; press.

Side border.
Make 2.

7. Sew the 2" x 30½" black print border strips to the top and bottom of the quilt. Press the seams toward the newly added borders. Sew the 2" x 33½" black print border strips to the sides; press.

Finishing the Quilt

Refer to "Finishing" on page 75 as needed to complete the quilt.

1. Piece the backing as needed. Layer the quilt top with batting and backing; baste.

2. Machine or hand quilt as desired.

3. Square up the quilt "sandwich." Use the 2½"-wide black print strips to bind the quilt edges. Finish by adding a label to the back of the quilt.

Quilt plan

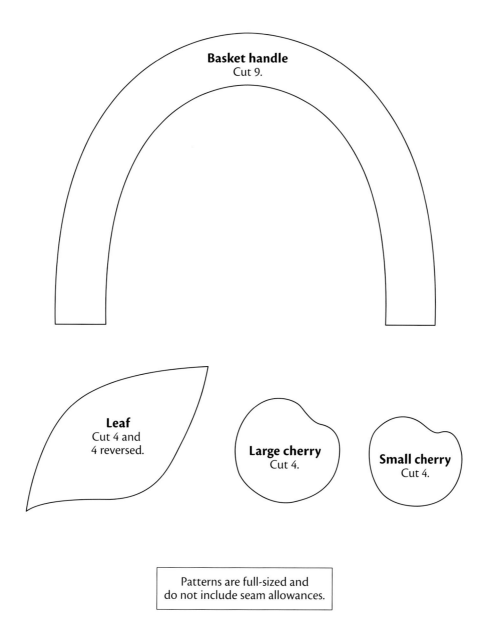

Basket handle
Cut 9.

Leaf
Cut 4 and
4 reversed.

Large cherry
Cut 4.

Small cherry
Cut 4.

Patterns are full-sized and
do not include seam allowances.

BALI High

Assorted batiks in sumptuous jewel tones, coupled with a simple block to showcase them, make this quilt as luscious as the evening skies over Bali.

Materials

Yardage is based on 42"-wide fabric.

3⅜ yards *total* of assorted tone-on-tone jewel-tone batiks for blocks

3⅜ yards *total* of assorted multicolored print batiks for blocks

⅔ yard of bluish green batik for binding

4½ yards of fabric for backing

78" x 78" piece of batting

Cutting

Measurements include ¼" seam allowances. Cut all strips on the crosswise grain (selvage to selvage).

From the assorted tone-on-tone jewel-tone batiks, cut a *total* of:

32 squares, 4½" x 4½"

64 rectangles, 2½" x 4½", in matching pairs*

64 rectangles, 2½" x 8½", in matching pairs*

34 squares, 2½" x 2½"

68 rectangles, 1½" x 2½", in matching pairs**

68 rectangles, 1½" x 4½", in matching pairs**

From the assorted multicolored print batiks, cut a *total* of:

32 squares, 4½" x 4½"

64 rectangles, 2½" x 4½", in matching pairs+

64 rectangles, 2½" x 8½", in matching pairs+

34 squares, 2½" x 2½"

68 rectangles, 1½" x 2½", in matching pairs++

68 rectangles, 1½" x 4½", in matching pairs++

From the bluish green batik, cut:

8 strips, 2½" x 42"

Cut these in matching sets of two rectangles, 2½" x 4½", and two rectangles, 2½" x 8½".

**Cut these in matching sets of two rectangles, 1½" x 2½", and two rectangles, 1½" x 4½".*

+*Cut these in matching sets of two rectangles, 2½" x 4½", and two rectangles, 2½" x 8½".*

++*Cut these in matching sets of two rectangles, 1½" x 2½", and two rectangles, 1½" x 4½".*

Making the Blocks

1. Sew a 4½" multicolored square between two matching 2½" x 4½" jewel-tone rectangles as shown; press. Make 32.

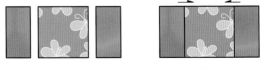

Make 32.

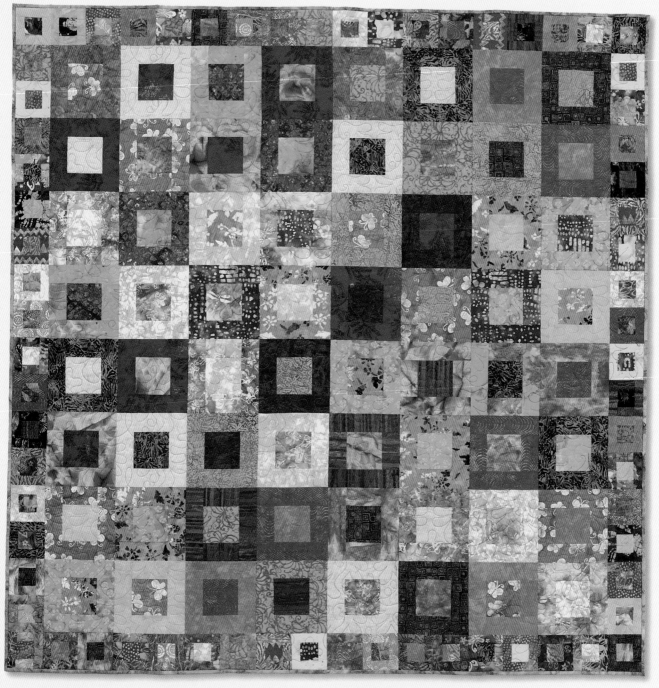

Quilted by Sharon Dixon
Finished quilt size: 72½" x 72½" • Finished block sizes: 8" x 8" and 4" x 4"

2. Sew matching 2½" x 8½" jewel-tone rectangles to the top and bottom of each unit from step 1; press. Square up the block to 8½" x 8½". Make 32 blocks and label them block A.

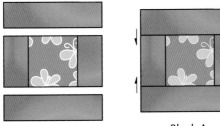

Block A.
Make 32.

3. Sew a 4½" jewel-tone square between two matching 2½" x 4½" multicolored rectangles as shown; press. Make 32.

Make 32.

4. Sew matching 2½" x 8½" multicolored rectangles to the top and bottom of each unit from step 3; press. Square up the block to 8½" x 8½". Make 32 blocks and label them block B.

Block B.
Make 32.

5. Repeat steps 1 and 2 using the 2½" multicolored squares and the 1½" x 2½" and 1½" x 4½" jewel-tone rectangles; press. Square up the blocks to 4½" x 4½". Make 34 and label them block C.

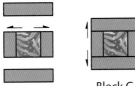

Block C.
Make 34.

6. Repeat steps 3 and 4 using the 2½" jewel-tone squares and the 1½" x 2½" and 1½" x 4½" multicolored rectangles; press. Square up the blocks to 4½" x 4½". Make 34 and label them block D.

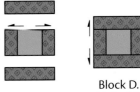

Block D.
Make 34.

Assembling the Quilt

1. Arrange blocks A and B in eight horizontal rows of eight blocks each, alternating them as shown in the assembly diagram. Rotate each A block 90° so that the 2½ " x 8½" strips of the A blocks appear on the left and right sides rather than on the top and bottom.

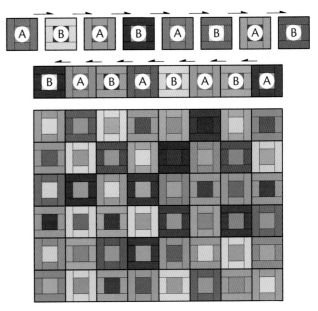

Assembly diagram

2. Sew the blocks together into rows; press.

3. Pin and sew the rows together, carefully matching the seams; press.

Adding the Borders

1. Arrange eight each of block C and block D, alternating them as shown. Rotate each D block 90° so that the 1½" x 4½" strips of the D blocks appear on the left and right sides rather than on the top and bottom. Sew the blocks together and press to make a side border. Make two. Sew the borders to the left and right edges of the quilt. Press the seams away from the borders.

Side border.
Make 2.

2. Arrange nine each of block C and block D, alternating them as shown. Rotate each D block 90° so that the 1½" x 4½" strips of the D blocks appear on the left and right sides rather than on the top and bottom. Sew the blocks together and press. Make two. Sew the borders to the top and bottom of the quilt; press.

Top/bottom border.
Make 2.

Finishing the Quilt

Refer to "Finishing" on page 75 as needed to complete the quilt.

1. Piece the backing as needed. Layer the quilt top with batting and backing; baste.

2. Machine or hand quilt as desired.

3. Square up the quilt "sandwich." Use the 2½"-wide bluish green strips to bind the quilt edges. Finish by adding a label to the back of the quilt.

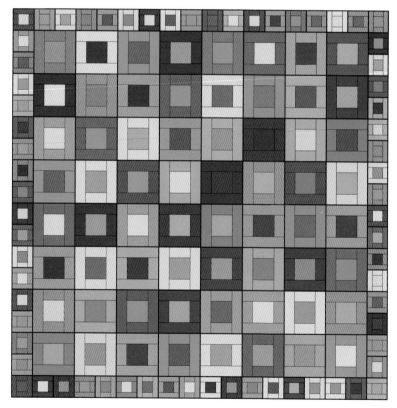

Quilt plan

Double-Pink BLOOMS

A selection of spring greens and double-pink reproduction prints give this quilt a sweet, romantic look. Add an old-world-style basket filled with pastel flowers and you have a quilt that is timeless.

Materials

Yardage is based on 42"-wide fabric unless otherwise noted. Fat quarters measure 18" x 22".

2½ yards of pink stripe for borders and binding

1⅝ yards of red-and-green border stripe for inner border

1 yard *total* of assorted light-value green prints for star backgrounds

1 yard *total* of assorted double-pink prints for sashing

⅞ yard of green check for basket backgrounds

¾ yard *total* of assorted dark-value, small-scale prints for star points

½ yard of pink paisley for baskets

½ yard *total* of assorted medium-value prints for triangles around star centers

⅓ yard *total* of assorted medium-scale floral prints for star centers

Fat quarter of blue print for flowers

Fat quarter of green print for stems

Fat quarter *each* of 2 green prints for pieced leaves

10" x 10" square of red print for hearts

6" x 6" scrap of yellow print for flower centers

3⅞ yards of fabric for backing (horizontal seam)

68" x 80" piece of batting

1 yard of lightweight fusible web

1 yard of tear-away stabilizer (optional)

⅝"-wide bias pressing bar

3" x 3" square of template plastic

Cutting

Measurements include ¼" seam allowances. Cut all strips on the crosswise grain (selvage to selvage) unless otherwise noted.

From the green check, cut:
2 strips, 13" x 42"; crosscut into 4 rectangles, 13" x 19"

From *each* green print for pieced leaves, cut:
2 strips, 2" x 22" (4 total)

From the fat quarter of green print for stems, cut:
1 strip, 4" x 22"

From the assorted double-pink prints, cut a *total* of:
69 squares, 3⅞" x 3⅞"; cut each square once diagonally to yield 138 half-square triangles

Quilted by Pam Klein
Finished quilt size: 60½" x 72½" • Finished block sizes: 12" x 18" and 6" x 6"

From the *lengthwise grain* of the red-and-green border stripe, cut:

2 strips, 2" x 43"

2 strips, 2" x 55"

From the assorted light-value green prints, cut a *total* of:

32 squares, 4¼" x 4¼"; cut each square twice diagonally to yield 128 quarter-square triangles in matching sets of 4*

128 squares, 2" x 2", in matching sets of 4*

From the assorted dark-value, small-scale prints, cut a *total* of:

128 squares, 2⅜" x 2⅜" in matching sets of 4; cut each square once diagonally to yield 256 half-square triangles in matching sets of 8

From the assorted medium-scale floral prints, cut a *total* of:

32 squares, 2⅝" x 2⅝"**

From the assorted medium-value prints, cut a *total* of:

64 squares, 2⅜" x 2⅜" in matching pairs; cut each square once diagonally to yield 128 half-square triangles in matching sets of 4

From the pink stripe, cut:

8 strips, 6½" x 42"

2½"-wide bias strips to total approximately 280"+

Cut these in matching sets of four quarter-square triangles and four 2" squares.

**I made a 2⅝" x 2⅝" see-through plastic template to fussy cut these squares.*

+*Refer to "Cutting and Making Bias Strips," step 1, on page 72.*

Making the Basket Blocks

The background blocks have been cut ½" larger than necessary and will be trimmed to size when the appliqué is complete.

1. Fold each 13" x 19" checked rectangle in half vertically and horizontally to find the center of the block; finger-press.

2. Use the patterns on page 61 to make templates for the basket, heart, flower, and flower center.

Referring to "Fusible Appliqué" on page 71, use the pink paisley and fusible web to prepare four basket appliqués, the red print square and fusible web to prepare four heart appliqués, the blue print and fusible web to prepare 12 flower appliqués, and the yellow print square and fusible web to prepare 12 flower center appliqués for fusing. For the larger appliqués, trim the fusible web from the center of the shape, leaving ¼" of fusible web inside the traced shape.

3. Sew together one 2" x 22" strip of each green print for leaves to make a strip set as shown; press. Make two. Referring to "Fusible Appliqué," use the pattern on page 61 to make a template for the split leaf. Use the strip sets and fusible web to prepare 12 pieced leaves for fusing by centering the split leaf shape over the strip as shown.

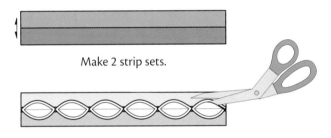

Make 2 strip sets.

4. Referring to "Fusible Appliqué," use fusible web to prepare the 4" x 22" green print strip for fusing. From the prepared strip, cut four strips, ½" x 8"; four strips, ½" x 5"; and four strips, ½" x 4". You will use these strips for stems in the next step.

5. Refer to the manufacturer's instructions to fuse one of each stem, one basket, one heart, three flowers, three flower centers, and three split leaves to each creased rectangle from step 1. Make four.

6. Pin a single layer of tear-away stabilizer to the back of each block. Make sure the stabilizer covers the entire area of the appliqué design. Finish the appliqué edges with matching thread and a machine buttonhole stitch. Remove the stabilizer, press, and trim each block to 12½" x 18½". If you prefer to use a hand buttonhole stitch, omit the stabilizer and refer to "Basic Embroidery Stitches" on page 75 as needed.

Assembling the Quilt

1. Sew the 3⅞" assorted double-pink half-square triangles together in pairs. Press the seams toward the darker fabric. Make 69.

Make 69.

2. Sew six units from step 1 together to make a row as shown; press. Make six.

Make 6.

3. Sew 11 units from step 1 together to make a row as shown; press. Make three.

Make 3.

4. Arrange and sew two Basket blocks and three units from step 2 together as shown; press. Make two.

5. Arrange the units from step 4 and the units from step 3, alternating them as shown in the assembly diagram. Sew the rows together; press. The quilt should measure 33½" x 45½".

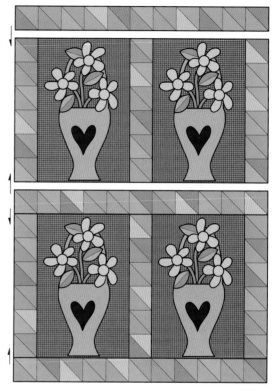

Assembly diagram

Adding the Inner Border

Referring to "Borders with Mitered Corners" on page 74 and the quilt plan on page 60, sew the 43"-long red-and-green striped inner-border strips to the top and bottom of the quilt and the 55"-long red-and-green striped inner-border strips to the sides; press. Miter the corners.

Making the Star Blocks

1. Sew matching 2⅜" dark print half-square triangles to the short edges of a 4¼" light green quarter-square triangle; press. Make four.

Make 4.

2. Sew matching 2⅜" medium-value print half-square triangles to opposite sides of a 2⅝" floral square; press. Repeat to add matching half-square triangles to the remaining sides; press.

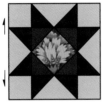

3. Arrange and sew the four units from step 1, the unit from step 2, and four matching 2" light green squares together in three rows as shown; press. Sew the rows together; press. Square up the block to 6½" x 6½".

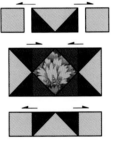

4. Repeat steps 1–3 to make a total of 32 blocks.

5. Sew eight blocks from step 4 together to make a border unit as shown; press. Make four.

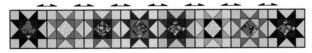

Make 4.

6. Referring to the quilt plan at right, sew a border unit from step 5 to the left and right edges of the quilt. Press the seams toward the quilt center. Sew the remaining border units to the top and bottom; press.

Adding the Outer Border

1. Sew the 6½" x 42" pink striped strips together end to end to form one long strip. Press the seams open. From this strip, cut two strips that measure 6½" x 68" and two strips that measure 6½" x 80".

2. Referring to "Borders with Mitered Corners" on page 74 and the quilt plan below, sew the 68"-long borders to the top and bottom of the quilt and the 80"-long borders to the sides; press. Miter the corners.

Finishing the Quilt

Refer to "Finishing" on page 75 as needed to complete the quilt.

1. Piece the backing as needed. Layer the quilt top with batting and backing; baste.

2. Machine or hand quilt as desired.

3. Square up the quilt "sandwich." Use the 2½"-wide pink striped strips to bind the quilt edges. Finish by adding a label to the back of the quilt.

Quilt plan

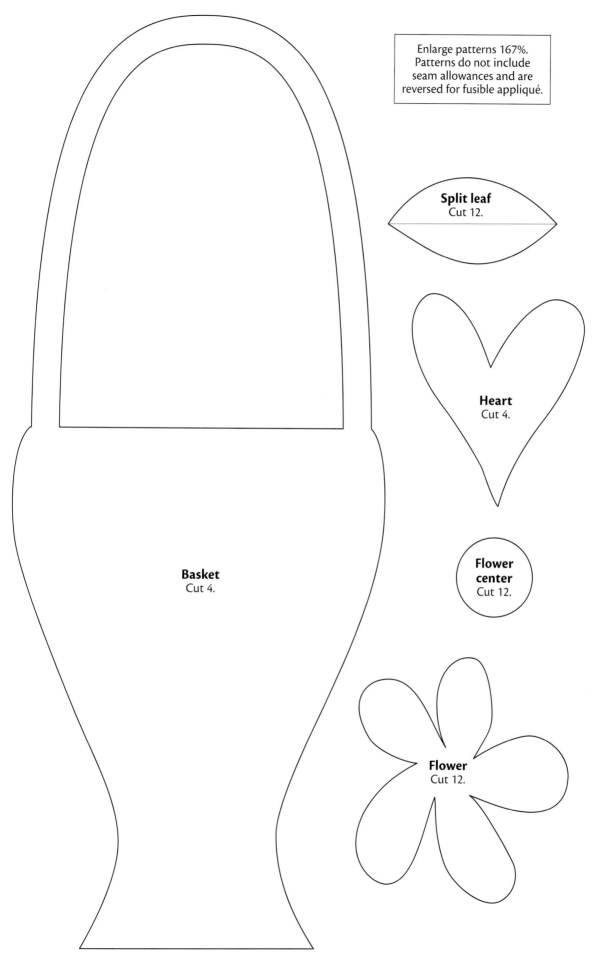

Enlarge patterns 167%.
Patterns do not include
seam allowances and are
reversed for fusible appliqué.

Split leaf
Cut 12.

Heart
Cut 4.

Flower center
Cut 12.

Basket
Cut 4.

Flower
Cut 12.

RAZZLE-DAZZLE Cactus Baskets

This colorful quilt is the result of a block exchange with ladies who live hundreds of miles away. What a great opportunity—and challenge—to use bright fabric scraps and the multitude of black-and-white prints that are currently so popular. The scrappy block is traditionally called Cake Stand, but it certainly looks like a basket to me!

Materials

Yardage is based on 42"-wide fabric unless otherwise noted. Fat eighths measure 9" x 22".

2⅞ yards of black print for alternate blocks, setting triangles, and outer border

⅝ yard of black-and-white small-scale check for middle border

½ yard *each* of 6 assorted white-with-black prints

⅓ yard *each* of white and red solid for pieced border

Fat eighth *each* of 12 assorted bright small-scale prints for basket points

Fat eighth *each* of 12 assorted bright prints for baskets

Fat eighth *each* of 12 assorted bright medium-scale prints for inside basket

¾ yard of black-with-white dotted print for binding

5 yards of fabric for backing (vertical seam)

71" x 88" piece of batting

2¼ yards *each* of 2 colors of jumbo rickrack

1¾ yards *each* of 2 colors of jumbo rickrack

Cutting

Measurements include ¼" seam allowances. Cut all strips on the crosswise grain (selvage to selvage).

From each white-with-black print, cut:

2 strips, 2⅜" x 42"; crosscut into 16 squares, 2⅜" x 2⅜". Cut each square once diagonally to yield 32 half-square triangles (192 total).

3 strips, 2" x 42" (18 total); crosscut into:
8 squares, 2" x 2" (48 total)
16 rectangles, 2" x 3½" (96 total)

4 squares, 3⅞" x 3⅞"; cut each square once diagonally to yield 8 half-square triangles (48 total)

From *each* fat eighth of assorted bright small-scale prints, cut:

8 squares, 2⅜" x 2⅜"; cut each square once diagonally to yield 16 half-square triangles (192 total)

From *each* fat eighth of assorted bright medium-scale prints, cut:

2 squares, 3⅞" x 3⅞"; cut each square once diagonally to yield 4 half-square triangles (48 total)

Quilted by Sharon Dixon
Finished quilt size: 63½" x 80½" • Finished block size: 6" x 6"

From *each* fat eighth of assorted bright print, cut:
2 squares, 3⅞" x 3⅞"; cut each square once diagonally to yield 4 half-square triangles (48 total)

4 squares, 2⅜" x 2⅜"; cut each square once diagonally to yield 8 half-square triangles (96 total)

From *each* of the white and red solid fabrics, cut:
6 strips, 1½" x 42" (12 total)

From the black-and-white small-scale check, cut:
7 strips, 2½" x 42"

From the black print, cut:
6 strips, 6½" x 42"; crosscut into 35 squares, 6½" x 6½"

2 strips, 9¾" x 42"; crosscut into 6 squares, 9¾" x 9¾". Cut each square twice diagonally to yield 24 quarter-square triangles.

2 squares, 5⅛" x 5⅛"; cut each square once diagonally to yield 4 half-square triangles

7 strips, 3½" x 42"

From the black-with-white dotted print, cut:
8 strips, 2½" x 42"

Making the Blocks

1. Sew a 2⅜" white-with-black half-square triangle and a 2⅜" small-scale print half-square triangle together to make a half-square-triangle unit as shown; press. Make 192 in matching sets of four.

Make 48
matching sets
of 4 (192 total).

2. Sew matching half-square-triangle units from step 1 together in pairs as shown; press. Make 48 of each.

Make 48 of each.

3. Sew a 3⅞" medium-scale print half-square triangle and a 3⅞" bright print half-square triangle together as shown; press. Make 48.

Make 48.

4. Arrange one of each unit from step 2, a unit from step 3, and a 2" matching white-with-black print square as shown. Sew the units and square together into rows; press. Sew the rows together; press. Make 48.

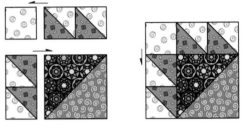

Make 48.

5. Matching both fabrics to a unit from step 4, sew a 2⅜" bright print half-square triangle to a 2" x 3½" white-with black print rectangle as shown; press. Make 48 of each.

Make 48 of each.

6. Sew one of each unit from step 5 to the matching unit from step 4 as shown; press. Make 48.

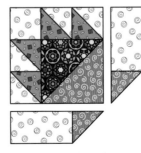
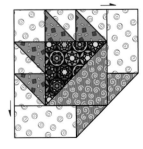

Make 48.

7. Finger-press the center of each 3⅞" white-with-black half-square triangle. Match the center of a creased triangle with the bottom center of a matching unit from step 6; pin. Sew and press. Square up the block to 6½" x 6½". Make 48 blocks.

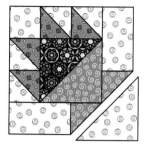 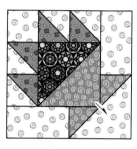

Make 48.

Assembling the Quilt

1. Arrange the Basket blocks, the 6½" black print squares, and the large black print side (quarter-square) and corner (half-square) setting triangles in diagonal rows as shown in the assembly diagram. Sew the blocks, squares, and triangles together into rows; press.

2. Pin and sew the rows together, carefully matching the seams; press.

Assembly diagram

Adding the Borders

1. Sew three 1½"-wide red strips and three 1½"-wide white strips together to make a strip set as shown; press. Make two. Cut the strip sets into 42 segments, 1½" wide.

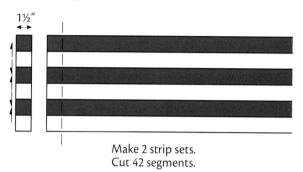

Make 2 strip sets.
Cut 42 segments.

Making Straight Strip Sets

When I make strip sets that will be crosscut into segments, I like to work with shorter strip lengths. If the strips are 42" long, I cut them into two or three equal lengths and then sew the strip set. When pressing, the seams remain straight and have less tendency to curve or bow.

2. Sew nine segments from step 1 together end to end; press. Make two inner-border units. For the top inner border, remove three squares (white, red, and white) from one end of the border unit as shown. For the bottom inner border, remove a red square from one end of the row and two squares (red and white) from the other end as shown.

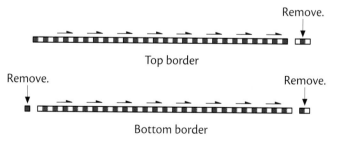

Remove.

Top border

Remove.   Remove.

Bottom border

3. Sew 12 segments from step 1 together to make a side inner-border unit; press. Make two. Remove two squares from each one of each border unit as shown.

Remove.

Side border.
Make 2.

4. Referring to the quilt plan at lower right, sew the border units from step 2 to the top and bottom of the quilt. Press the seams toward the quilt center. Sew the border units from step 3 to the sides; press. The quilt top should measure 53½" x 70½".

5. Sew the 2½"-wide checked border strips together end to end to make one long strip. From this strip, cut two strips that measure 2½" x 53½" and two strips that measure 2½" x 74½".

6. Sew the 2½" x 53½" strips to the top and bottom of the quilt. Press the seams toward the newly added borders. Sew the 2½" x 74½" strips to the sides; press. The quilt top should measure 57½" x 74½".

7. Sew the 3½"-wide black print border strips together end to end to make one long strip. From this strip, cut two strips that measure 3½" x 57½" and two strips that measure 3½" x 80½".

8. Sew the 3½" x 57½" strips to the top and bottom of the quilt. Press the seams toward the newly added borders. Sew the 2½" x 80½" strips to the sides; press. The quilt top should measure 63½" x 80½".

9. Cut two 57½"-long strips of rickrack, one each from the two shorter lengths of rickrack. Repeat to cut a 74½"-long strip of rickrack from each of the remaining colors. Center a 74½"-long strip of rickrack on the seam between the middle and outer borders on the right side of the quilt. Use matching thread to topstitch in place. Repeat to add a 57½"-long piece of rickrack to the bottom, the remaining 74½"-long piece to the left, and the remaining

57½"-long piece to the top, turning under any raw edges as shown. Press the quilt top.

Finishing the Quilt

Refer to "Finishing" on page 75 as needed to complete the quilt.

1. Piece the backing as needed. Layer the quilt top with batting and backing; baste.

2. Machine or hand quilt as desired.

3. Square up the quilt "sandwich." Use the 2½"-wide dotted print strips to bind the quilt edges. Finish by adding a label to the back of the quilt.

Quilt plan

Quiltmaking Basics

The following pages outline the various techniques you'll need to know to successfully complete the quilts in this book. Refer to them as needed as you work on each project.

Tools of the Trade

The following list will help you gather all the essential tools for these projects.

- Sewing machine in good working order, preferably equipped with a ¼" presser-foot attachment
- 70/10 or 80/12 needles for machine piecing, size 11 Sharps for hand appliqué, and chenille #24 for buttonhole appliqué
- Good-quality, all-cotton or cotton-covered polyester thread
- Rotary cutter, medium size (45mm)
- Self-healing cutting mat (24" x 38")
- See-through rulers in varying widths and lengths
- Square rulers, from 2" to 16"
- Sharp fabric scissors, small pointed-tip scissors for appliqué and clipping threads, and crafter's scissors for cutting plastic templates and paper-foundation pieces
- Seam ripper to remove stitches
- Bias pressing bars in varying widths
- Clear or frosted template plastic to make durable, accurate templates
- Sandpaper board to hold fabric in place as you mark it (optional)

Rotary Cutting

The projects in this book include instructions for quick and easy rotary cutting whenever possible. All measurements include standard ¼"-wide seam allowances unless otherwise indicated. For those unfamiliar with rotary cutting, a brief introduction is provided below. For more detailed information, see *The Quilter's Quick Reference Guide* by Candace Eisner Strick (Martingale & Company, 2004).

The following instructions are for right-handed quilters. Reverse the procedure if you are left-handed.

1. Fold the fabric, matching the selvages and aligning the crosswise and lengthwise grains as much as possible. Place the fabric with the folded edge closest to you on the cutting mat. Align a square ruler along the folded edge of the fabric, and then place a long, straight acrylic ruler to the left of the square, just covering the uneven raw edges on the left edge of the fabric.

2. Remove the square ruler and cut along the right edge of the long ruler, rolling the rotary cutter away from you. Discard this strip.

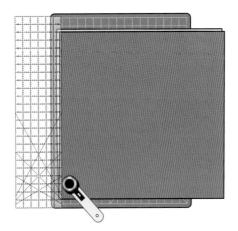

3. To cut strips, align the required measurement on the ruler with the newly cut edge of the fabric. For example, to cut a 3"-wide strip, place the 3" mark of your ruler on the edge of the fabric.

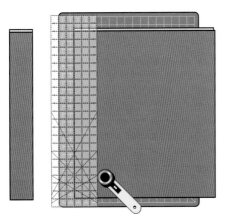

4. To cut squares, cut strips in the required widths. Trim away the selvage ends. Align the required measurement on the ruler with the left edge of the strip and cut a square. Continue cutting squares until you have the number needed.

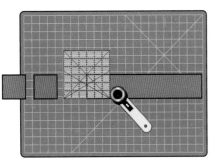

5. To cut half-square triangles from squares, place a square (or layered stack of squares) on your cutting mat. Position your ruler diagonally over the square, with the cutting edge aligned directly over the corners, and make the cut.

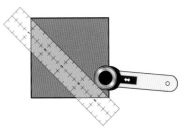

6. To cut quarter-square triangles, place a square (or layered stack of squares) on your cutting mat. Position your ruler diagonally over the square, with the cutting edge aligned directly over the corners, and make the cut. Without shifting the fabrics, reposition your ruler and make a diagonal cut from corner to corner in the opposite direction.

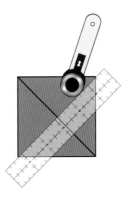

Machine Piecing

The most important aspect of machine piecing is to sew with an accurate ¼" seam allowance. A ¼" presser-foot attachment is an invaluable tool. It takes all the guesswork out of sewing an accurate ¼"-wide seam. On some machines, you can move the needle position to the left or right so that the distance between the needle and the edge of the presser foot is ¼".

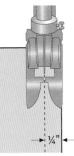

If your machine doesn't have either of these features, you can create a seam guide by measuring and then placing a piece of tape or moleskin ¼" to the right of the needle.

For regular (not foundation) piecing, set your machine stitch length at approximately 10 to 12 stitches per inch. Line up the cut edges of your fabric pieces precisely and stitch. Backstitching is not necessary, since eventually the seams will be crossed by other seams.

Chain piecing saves you both time and thread, and it is an especially efficient method if you are sewing multiples of identical units. To chain piece, sew your first pair of patches together. At the end of the seam line, stop sewing but do not cut the thread. Feed the next pair of patches under the presser foot and continue sewing in the same manner until all the patches are sewn. Remove the chain of sewn patches from the machine and clip the threads between the sewn units.

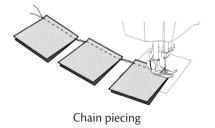

Chain piecing

If you need to sew two patches or units together that are slightly different in size, pin the pieces together, matching the key points and edges and distributing the fullness evenly by adding more pins if necessary. Sew the seam with the larger piece of fabric underneath. The feed dogs will ease the bottom fabric to fit.

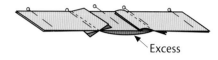

Excess

Measure As You Go

Fabrics can shift a bit when you piece triangles together. Always take the time to press and measure the units as you go and make any adjustments as needed. If you do this after each step, your blocks will be more accurate.

I am a real taskmaster when it comes to pressing and always recommend that you press the seams as you go. (Besides improving the accuracy of your piecing, this gives you an excuse to get up from the sewing machine for a little exercise.) Plan your pressing so that seams in adjacent units are pressed in opposite directions. I've included pressing arrows in the instructions for each project. As a general rule, press seams open when working with a block that is 4" square or smaller. The block will be much flatter and less bulky.

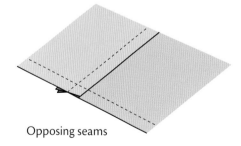

Opposing seams

Making Templates for Appliqué

Templates made from clear plastic are more durable and accurate than those made from cardboard. Since you can see through the plastic, it also is easy to fussy cut a desired motif.

The project instructions for each quilt tell you whether the appliqués are done using the freezer-paper hand method (below) or using fusible web (page 71). The patterns are oriented for the specific project instructions, but you can adapt them to your preferred method if you wish.

To make a template, place the template plastic over each appliqué pattern piece and trace with a fine-line permanent marker. Cut out the templates directly on the drawn lines. You need only one template for each different motif or shape. Mark the pattern name on the template.

Freezer-Paper Hand Appliqué

I prefer the freezer-paper method for hand appliqué. To adapt a fusible pattern for freezer paper, simply reverse the pattern.

1. Place the freezer paper shiny side down on the pattern and use a pencil to trace the shape. If you have made plastic templates, you can use them for tracing the designs. Cut out the design on the pencil line; do not add seam allowances to the freezer paper. To cut reversed shapes, simply turn your plastic template over and trace the reverse pattern.

2. Place the freezer-paper template shiny side down on the right side of the appliqué fabric. Press with a hot, dry iron for one to two seconds. Cut out the fabric shape, adding a ¼" seam allowance around the outside edge of the freezer paper.

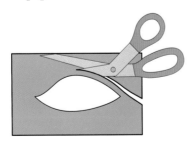

Cut ¼" from edge
of freezer paper.

3. Carefully peel off the freezer paper and center it shiny side up on the wrong side of the fabric. Use the tip of your iron to press the fabric seam allowance over the edge of the freezer paper. Be careful not to shift the paper as you go. Fold the outside points as shown.

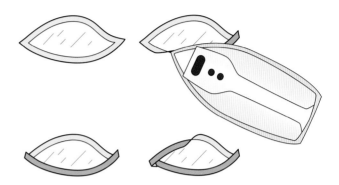

4. Clip any inside curves as shown to prevent puckering. This is a must for the basket handle patterns in this book.

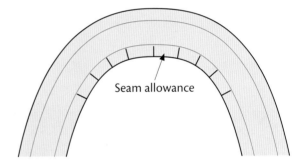

Seam allowance

5. Pin the prepared appliqués in place on the background fabric and thread baste. As an alternative, pin baste with short appliqué pins so your thread won't get caught as you stitch.

6. Use a small blind hem stitch and matching thread to stitch each appliqué in place. Begin with the pieces that will be overlapped by other pieces and layer as you go. Tuck in the seam allowances on points as you come to them.

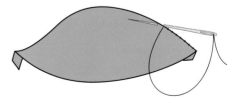

7. Remove the basting stitches or pins. Working from the back, use small, sharp scissors to cut a ½" slit in the background fabric behind the appliqué. Be careful not to cut into the appliquéd piece. Use tweezers to carefully remove the freezer paper. (You may need to tug a little if you have stitched through the paper.) When you are finished, press the block.

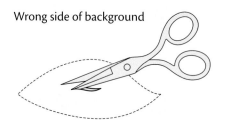

Wrong side of background

Fusible Appliqué

Fusible appliqué is fast and easy; there are no seams to turn under. Simply fuse and stitch. While it is not my choice for heirloom-style quilts (for example, a Baltimore Album quilt), it is a good choice for many quilt projects, including many projects in this book. To adapt a freezer-paper pattern for fusible appliqué, simply reverse the pattern.

Choose lightweight, sewable fusible web and always read the manufacturer's instructions before you begin. Fusible web has smooth paper on one side, with an adhesive on the reverse side. If you are planning to hand stitch your project, choose the most lightweight fusible web you can find. This is especially important if you will be hand stitching through multiple layers.

You can reduce the bulk and stiffness of fused appliqués by cutting away all but ¼" of the fusible web inside the traced lines. This allows the shape to adhere to the background fabric but eliminates the stiffness of the adhesive within the shape.

With fusible appliqué, you will draw or trace your templates in reverse of how they will appear in the finished quilt. Use a light box or tape the pattern and the template material to a bright window for this task.

1. Use a pencil to trace around the appliqué pattern (or template) on the paper side of the fusible web.

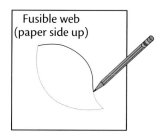

Fusible web
(paper side up)

2. Cut the shape from the fusible web, leaving approximately ¼" outside the traced lines. If the shape is large, cut the fusible from inside the shape as well, leaving a ¼" margin inside the traced line.

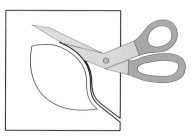

3. Place the fusible-web shape adhesive side down on the wrong side of the appliqué fabric. Follow the manufacturer's instructions to press the shape to the fabric. Let the fabric and adhesive cool.

4. Cut out the fabric shape on the drawn line and remove the paper from the fusible web.

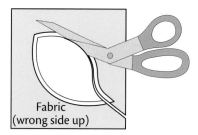

Fabric
(wrong side up)

5. Using your pattern as a guide, position the appliqué shape, with the newly exposed adhesive side down, on the right side of the background fabric; press. I like to place the entire motif (for example, all flower parts) on

the background and press just once. If you press a shape over and over, the adhesive will melt and the appliqué won't stick.

6. When all the pieces in the block or design are fused, finish the edges with hand or machine decorative stitches.

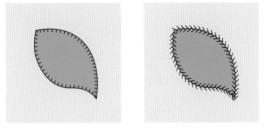

Cutting and Making Bias Strips

1. Align the 45° mark on your rotary ruler with the bottom edge of the fabric as shown. Use a rotary cutter to cut the required number of strips in the widths specified in the project instructions.

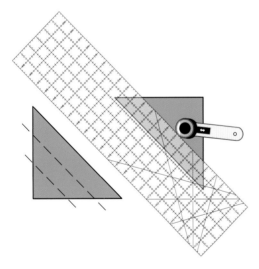

2. Fold each strip in half lengthwise, wrong sides together, and stitch from the folded edge as specified in the project instructions. Trim the seam allowance as directed.

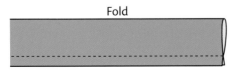

Fold

3. Insert a bias pressing bar of the desired width, roll the fabric tube so the seam is centered along one flat edge of the bias bar, and press. Remove the bias bar.

Bias bar

Squaring Up Blocks

Always take the time to press, measure, and square up your quilt blocks. This is especially true in exchange quilts. Everyone sews with a slightly different seam allowance. Blocks of different sizes can cause havoc when it's time to piece the quilt top.

Use a large square ruler to measure your blocks and make sure they are the desired size, plus an exact ¼" on each edge for seam allowance. If your blocks vary slightly in size, trim the larger blocks to match the size of the smallest one if it is possible to do so without chopping off any points. Not all blocks can be trimmed to fit; you may need to make slight adjustments in block seams. Be sure to trim all four sides; otherwise, your block will be lopsided.

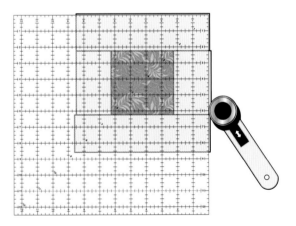

Quilt Top Assembly

Lay out the blocks in horizontal or diagonal rows as indicated in the project instructions. Evaluate the layout for balance of color, repositioning blocks as necessary or even making substitutions to achieve the look that you desire. Once you are satisfied with the arrangement, you are ready to assemble the quilt top.

In most cases you will press block seams in alternating directions from row to row so the seams butt together when joined. When assembling large tops, begin by joining the rows in groups of two or three. Then, beginning from opposite sides of the quilt, join the grouped rows into larger sections until you join the two halves. I especially like this technique when I am piecing diagonal rows.

Keeping Order

To keep your blocks in their proper positions as you assemble the quilt top, label them with adhesive dots marked with the row and block numbers, such as 1-1, 1-2, 1-3; 2-1, 2-2, 2-3; and so on. You'll find these dots at any office-supply store.

Borders

I find adding borders to be the most challenging part of the entire quiltmaking process. Pieced borders require extra attention to ensure that they fit the quilt properly. Borders that are too long can appear ruffled, while borders that are too short can cause puckered areas in the quilt center. You may need to adjust the border measurements in this book to allow for differences in your personal piecing process.

BORDERS WITH SQUARED CORNERS

Usually I add the side borders and then the top and bottom borders, but occasionally I add them in reverse order. Refer to the individual projects for guidance as needed.

1. Measure the length of the quilt top through the center. Cut two border strips to that measurement, piecing as necessary. Mark the centers of the quilt edges and the border strips by finger-pressing or inserting a pin. Pin the borders to the sides of the quilt top,

matching the center marks and ends and easing as necessary. Sew the border strips in place. Press the seams toward the border unless directed otherwise.

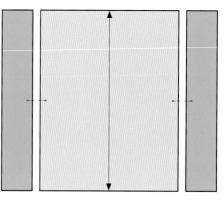

Measure center of quilt, top to bottom.
Mark centers.

2. Measure the width of the quilt top through the center, including the side borders just added. Cut two border strips to that measurement, piecing if necessary. Mark the center of the quilt edges and the border strips. Pin the borders to the top and bottom edges of the quilt top, matching the center marks and ends and easing as necessary. Stitch the borders to the quilt; press.

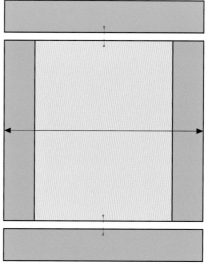

Measure center of quilt, side to side.
Mark centers.

BORDERS WITH MITERED CORNERS

Mitered borders add a nice finished touch to a quilt top and are best used when matching border prints and stripes. I also enjoy mitering when I use multiple borders.

Mitering Multiple Borders

When I'm adding multiple borders to my quilt and plan to miter the corners, I sew the border strips together first to create a border unit. Then I only need to miter each corner once rather than many times.

1. Find the center of one border strip and the appropriate side of the quilt top. With right sides together, align marked midpoints and pin the border to the quilt, allowing the excess border fabric to extend equally beyond the quilt top edges. Stitch the border to the quilt top, starting and stopping ¼" from each corner with a backstitch. Repeat with the remaining borders.

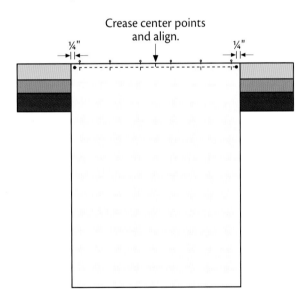

2. Working one corner at a time, fold the quilt top right sides together at a 45° angle. Align the edges of adjacent borders, match any border seam lines, and pin through all the layers about 3" from the border corner. Place a ruler along the fold and extend the length across the border strips, aligning the 45° mark of the ruler with the border's edge.

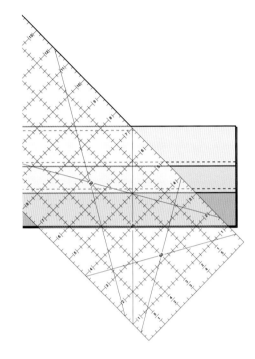

3. Draw a line along the ruler from the outer edge of the border to the seam line. Pin the border strips as shown and sew on the marked line.

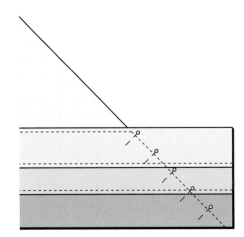

4. Trim the seam allowance to ¼" and press the seam open. Repeat for the remaining corners.

Basic Embroidery Stitches

Use these basic hand stitches to add detail and texture to your quilts.

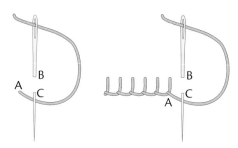

Blanket stitch or buttonhole stitch

Running stitch

Stem stitch

Finishing

Quilt tops can be marked in many ways, depending upon the look you wish to achieve and the style of your quilt. If you plan to outline appliqués or if you plan to stitch in the ditch (along the seam line), it may not be necessary to mark the quilting pattern. ("Mark as little as possible" is my motto.) You can use masking tape to mark backgrounds for grids or cross-hatching; just be sure to remove the tape at the end of every day. More elaborate designs should be marked on the quilt top with a removable fine-tipped marking tool. *Always* test your marking tool to make sure you can remove the marks easily.

BATTING

There are many types of batting available and each one gives your quilt a different look. For hand quilting, I prefer wool batting. Otherwise, an 80/20 batting is my batting of choice for most quilts. I typically cut the batting a few inches larger than the quilt top on all sides.

BACKING

When you choose your backing fabric, remember that busy-looking prints will make your quilting stitches less visible, while tone-on-tone prints will emphasize your stitches and quilt designs.

I cut and seam my quilt backings to be 4" larger than the quilt top on all sides. Larger quilts may require a pieced back. It is acceptable to place the seams vertically or horizontally—whichever requires fewer seams and makes more economical use of fabric. Trim all selvages before sewing the seams for the backing, and sew the pieces together with a ⅝"-wide seam. Press the seams open to reduce bulk.

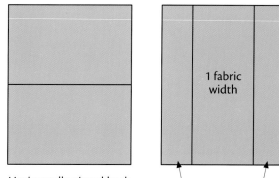

Horizontally pieced back

Partial fabric width

1 fabric width

Making a scrappy backing—also called "back art"—is another option you might try. These backings can be fun when made from leftover fabrics or blocks from the quilt top. If you need only a few more inches of fabric, consider adding a different piece of fabric to the back. Be aware, however, that the additional layers of fabric at every seam can make hand quilting difficult.

BASTING

1. Place the backing fabric, wrong side up, on a large, flat surface. Smooth away any wrinkles and use masking tape to secure it in place.

2. Layer the batting over the secured backing fabric, centering it and smoothing away any wrinkles.

3. Center the quilt top, right side up, over the first two layers. Baste in place from corner to corner, and then in a vertical and horizontal grid, spacing the rows about 3" to 4" apart. If you intend to hand quilt, use a long needle and a light-colored thread. For machine quilting, use small, rustproof safety pins.

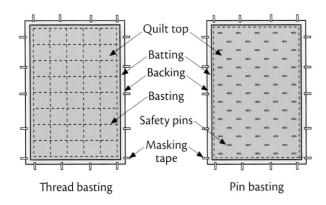

Thread basting   Pin basting

HAND QUILTING

To quilt by hand, you will need short, sturdy needles (called "Betweens"), quilting thread, and a thimble to fit the middle finger of your sewing hand. Many quilters also use a frame or hoop to support their work. Use the smallest needle you can comfortably handle; the finer the needle, the smaller the stitches will be.

1. Thread your needle with a single strand of quilt thread, approximately 18" long. Make a small knot and insert the needle in the top layer about 1" from the place where you want to start stitching. Pull the needle out at the point where quilting will begin and gently pull the thread until the knot pops through the fabric and into the batting.

2. Begin with a small backstitch and then make small, evenly spaced stitches through all three layers. Rock the needle up and down through all layers until you have three or four stitches on the needle. Place your other hand underneath the quilt so you can feel the needlepoint with the tip of your finger when a stitch is taken.

3. To end a line of quilting, make a small knot close to the last stitch; then backstitch, running the thread a needle's length through the batting. Gently pull the thread until the knot pops into the batting. Clip the thread at the quilt's surface.

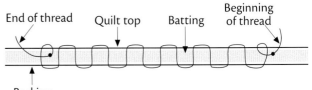

MACHINE QUILTING

Machine quilting is suitable for all types of quilts, from crib-size to full-size bed quilts. With machine quilting, you can complete your quilt tops quickly. If you are a purist, like I used to be, you might scoff at the idea of having anything of yours machine quilted. But wouldn't your children rather have finished quilts than tops? There just aren't enough hours in the day to hand quilt everything.

You might want to consider machine quilting a few quilt tops yourself or having a professional quilt them for you. If you choose to do them yourself, refer to *Machine Quilting Made Easy!* by Maurine Noble (Martingale & Company, 1994) for detailed, expert guidance.

For straight-line quilting, you need a walking foot to help feed the quilt layers through the machine without shifting or puckering. Some machines have a built-in walking foot; other machines require a separate attachment.

For free-motion quilting, you need a darning foot and the ability to drop the feed dogs on your machine. With free-motion quilting, you do not turn the fabric under the needle but instead guide the fabric in the direction of the design. Use free-motion quilting to outline quilt a pattern in the fabric or to create stippling or other curved designs.

BINDING

I prefer bias binding on most of my quilts, especially those with curved edges. I find it easier to work with, and the finished edges don't fray as easily. Strips cut on the crosswise grain (from selvage to selvage) across the width of the fabric can be used on straight-sided quilts and I have used them for some of the quilts in this book as well.

For a French double-fold binding—bias or straight—cut strips 2½" wide. You will need enough strips to go around the perimeter of the quilt, plus about 10" extra for seams and corners in a mitered fold. Refer to "Cutting and Making Bias Strips" page 72 for instructions on cutting bias strips for binding. The following steps work for either bias or straight strips.

1. With right sides together, join the strips as shown to make a single binding strip. Press the seams open.

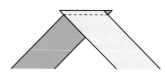

2. Fold the strip in half lengthwise, wrong sides together, and press.

3. Trim the excess batting and backing to ¼" beyond the raw edge of the quilt top. If you wish to add a hanging sleeve to your quilt, refer to "Adding a Hanging Sleeve" on page 78 and do so now.

4. Align the raw edges of the binding with the raw edges of the quilt top. Starting 10" from the end of the binding strip, in the middle of the bottom edge of the quilt top, use a

walking foot and a ¼"-wide seam allowance to stitch the binding to the quilt. End the stitching ¼" from the first corner and backstitch.

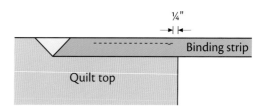

5. Turn the quilt so that you will be stitching down the next side. Fold the binding up, away from the quilt, with raw edges aligned. Fold the binding back down onto itself, even with the edge of the quilt top. Begin stitching at the edge of the quilt top, backstitching to secure. Repeat on the remaining edges and corners of the quilt.

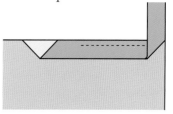

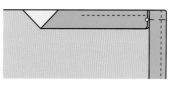

6. Stop stitching approximately 15" from the point at which you started sewing the binding to the quilt. Halfway between the starting and stopping points, cut the end of one strip at a 45° angle. Unfold both strips and lay the cut strip on top of the uncut strip. Cut the bottom strip at a 45° angle so that the strips overlap by ½" and the angles are both cut in the same direction.

7. With right sides together, stitch the cut ends of the binding with a ¼" seam as shown. Press the seam open and refold the binding. Finish stitching the binding to the quilt.

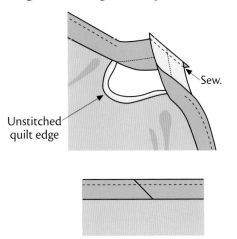

Sew.

Unstitched quilt edge

8. Fold the binding over the raw edges of the quilt to the back, with the folded edge covering the row of machine stitching. Use matching thread and a blind hem stitch to secure the binding in place. A miter will form at each corner. Stitch the mitered corners closed.

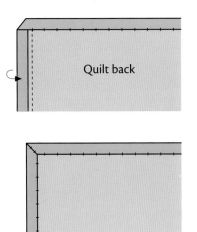

Quilt back

ADDING A HANGING SLEEVE

One of the simplest ways to hang your quilt is to attach a fabric sleeve to the back. I usually use the same fabric for the sleeve that I used for the backing. I also sew the sleeve on before the binding. Not every quilt needs a hanging sleeve—only the ones you wish to display on a wall or hang in a quilt show.

1. Cut a piece of fabric 8½" wide x the width of the quilt top *minus 2"*. Fold the short ends of the strip under and finish them with a straight stitch.

2. Fold the hemmed strip in half lengthwise, right sides out. Pin the two raw edges of the sleeve to the back of the quilt within ¼" of the raw edge of the quilt top, and machine baste the sleeve to the quilt with a scant ¼" seam. The edge of the sleeve will be covered when you attach the binding.

Sleeve

Quilt back

3. Hand stitch the folded edge to the quilt with a blind hem stitch, being careful not to go through the front of the quilt. Add the binding as described on page 77.

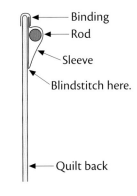

Binding
Rod
Sleeve
Blindstitch here.

Quilt back

LABELING YOUR QUILT

I do an entire lecture on labeling quilts. It is so important to write, type, or embroider a few facts about your quilt. Each quilt label should include certain basic information:

- Your full name, including your maiden name if you like

- Date the quilt was made. If it took two years, you can write: Started April 2004 – Finished 2006.

- Name of the quilt pattern

- Quilt dimensions (very helpful when entering it into a show)

- City and state where the quilt was made

- Who quilted it, if not you

- Any other details you want to include for posterity

Example of a simple handwritten label

About the Author

Cynthia LeBlanc Regone was born in the heart of Cajun country, in Lafayette, Louisiana. She and her husband have three children. She is a graduate of the University of Louisiana at Lafayette.

Besides playing in three different tennis leagues, this busy mom still finds time to pursue her passion for quilting, reading, "doing lunch with friends," and traveling.

Cynthia started quilting in 1981 and within 10 years was producing award-winning quilts. She lectures, teaches, and judges quilt shows throughout the United States. She has served on the board of several state and local guilds in Oklahoma and Texas. She was a featured teacher at the 31st Annual National Quilting Association Show in 2000 and teaches at the International Quilt Festival in Houston, Texas.

True to her roots, Cynthia designs under her own pattern label, Cajun Classics.